A Sweet
Oblation

Irma Silva-Barbeau, Ph.D.

Tate Publishing, LLC

Dedication

To LOVE

Acknowledgments

I am humbled by the process of producing this book. From a small idea that came to me almost three years ago, this book took shape mainly by the discussions with my family and listening to the stories and events that had captivated my imagination as a child.

I am in great debt to all my brothers and sisters, but especially to my brother Antonio Silva who read the very first draft and encouraged me to go on. I am indebted to my sisters, Adelaide Macêdo, Fernanda Oliveira, Manuela Silva, Celiza Leitão, and my brother John Silva who clarified for me the different aspects of life in Brava that I included in the book. I am grateful to my sister, Dr. Izione S. Silva, who provided insightful comments, and to my nieces, Jennifer Silva and Kathleen Macêdo for their much appreciated input.

In Blacksburg, I thank my daughters, Sarah and Rebecca, for listening enthusiastically to my every idea and for being my "gentle readers." My husband, Bill, I thank him for letting me dream and for taking care of business around the house when I was too preoccupied to do so.

I am in great debt to my friends who served as preliminary editors. A sincere thank you goes to Catherine Merola, who read draft after draft and served as key preliminary editor. Also, Emily Crawford, who in spite of having three small children, has been a steady supporter, preliminary editor, and commentator of my writings. I also thank my friend and neighbor, Beverly Kingston, for her encouragement and support. I am also grateful to members of my book discussion group, "Body, Mind and Spirit," whose wisdom and friendship have sustained me.

A special thank you goes to Tate Publishing for believing in my book and for publishing it.

Finally, I thank God, His angels, and saints for my life, family, friends, and inspiration to write.

Disclaimer

The views and opinions expressed in this book are those of the author. They do not represent the official views of the Roman Catholic Church. Furthermore, this is a work of historical fiction; but some real events, rituals, and traditions are presented. The author used her own family as model for the Rodrigues family; however, the individual characters are an amalgamation of characters derived from the author's imagination and do not represent fully any one real character. In addition, the interpretation of some of the events is the author's and may differ from those of readers familiar with the subject and/or with Capeverdian customs.

Contents

" . . . something as insignificant as a cookie can remind us that we all are pilgrims on our way. "[1]

---

[1] Fr. Benedict J. Groeschel, C.F.R. The King, Crucified and Risen–Meditations on the Passion and Glory of Christ–Daily readings from Ash Wednesday to Divine Mercy Sunday. Servant Publications, Ann Harbor, Michigan, 2002

Foreword

Curiosity, instinct, imagination, and courage lead Isabel, and each of us, to question God's ways, follow our guts, see the face of Jesus in others, and act on faith. Arguing with her mother, listening to the voice of the little girl within her, understanding that the outcasts are "just like us," and joyfully sacrificing small pleasures enable Isabel to grasp the paradox of the Paschal Mystery.

In her Lenten bridge between childhood and adulthood, Isabel recognizes the mob mentality of killing "evil" spiders on Good Friday and instead burns her private diary of sins stuffed inside her effigy of Judas. Her winged reward is imminent and immanent–the Good News revealed Easter Sunday in her front yard.

May Isabel's spiritual journey inspire each of us to daily serve the needy we encounter by feeding poor BaBa, complimenting the disabled Mr. Little Hands, praising the beggar Mr. Tallman, and asking the ill Miss Mary for her prayers. Isabel's gift to us is an invitation to penetrate the depth of reality, sing with the joy with our Protestant brothers and sisters, and incorporate the wisdom of the Spirit.

I hope that all readers will feel honored, as I have, to enter this story, live its mysteries, and know its graces. Indeed, *A Sweet Oblation* is a sweet oblation!

> January 2005
> (Rev.) Michael J. Ellerbrock, PhD
> Catholic Deacon
> Blacksburg, Virginia

Introduction

The story of *A Sweet Oblation* takes place on the island of Brava, in the archipelago of the Cape Verde Islands, West Africa, during the 1950s, some twenty years before the islands became independent from Portugal. This was nearly a decade before the Twenty-First Ecumenical Council of the Roman Catholic Church, also known as Vatican II.

Both events, the independence of the islands and Vatican II, brought dramatic changes to the normal day-to-day lives of families like the Rodrigueses, and that of the young protagonist, Isabel.

The lives of people in Brava, before these events, were dominated by the Church—dictated by the social, economic, and political structures that were put in place upon the Portuguese arrival on the islands in 1460.

Notwithstanding these events, by the 1950s, change was in the air. No corner of the world, not even the most remote and geopolitical insignificant

Brava, was left unchanged by the ghastly events of World War II.

The Catholic Church responded to that war by a renewed spirit of ecumenism that first began among some Protestants, and subsequently was embraced by the Catholic Church in Vatican II.[1] The Catholic Church responded to the "longing" of all Christians to unite, and recognized the necessity for greater involvement of the laity, as well as respecting the language, art, and music of various cultures as worthy means of expression in worship. Although Latin remains to this day the official language of the Church in Rome, the Catholic service, the Mass, which was conducted strictly in Latin, is now conducted in the vernacular, and the faithful are invited to participate more fully in the worship services. Vatican II also recognized the Church's responsibility towards all humanity irrespective of their faiths and creeds and saw the Church as "the people of God."

To understand the culture of the protagonist, Isabel, is to understand the culture of the Capeverdian that evolved since the islands were discovered. At the time of their discovery, the islands were not inhabited. The ten islands were grouped into the *Sotavento*, the southern islands, and the *Barlavento*, the northern islands. The *Sotavento* consists of the islands of Maio, São Tiago, Fogo (with an active volcano), and Brava. The *Barlavento* consists of the islands of Boa Vista, Sal, São Nicolau, Santa Luzia, São Vicente, and Santo Antão. The archipelago is situated about 300 nautical miles west of Senegal, West Africa.

The first settlers were feudal lords to whom the king of Portugal gave vast tracts of land in the newly discovered territories to settle and rule. In addition to the feudal lords, settlers came from the Algarve region of Portugal, and the island of Madeira. There were also Spaniards, Italians, and Jews. Africans were brought to the islands as slaves and the islands were active in the slave trade until it was outlawed.

Crioulo[2] was the language that was spoken in all occasions in the 1950s, and families like the Rodrigueses spoke Crioulo, to the exclusion of Portuguese. In some families, the men could speak some Portuguese, and children learned it in school.

The development of the Capeverdian Crioulo language and its adoption by the white settlers was a process by which settlers began to develop their own unique culture independent of the Portuguese and that of the African. The unique Capeverdean culture developed out of the islands' isolation from the world (also each island from the next), administrative neglect from Portugal, regular and destructive pirate attacks, and cyclic droughts and famines. This political and ecological setting is also responsible for the Capeverdian diaspora and the *sodade,* or the cultural longing, for the loved ones in foreign lands and of the mother country left behind.

In 1875 the population of Brava was boosted from the people of the neighboring island of Fogo who fled from a volcanic eruption. On Brava, the whites, finding the climate to their liking, prospered and multiplied. The world also had opened up to the residents of Brava, in the early nineteenth century through American whalers. The whalers found Brava's natural bays excellent shelters for their ships in stormy weather. Soon young men from Brava became regular crew members in these ships and the relationship with the United States began and blossomed; the impact of which is felt even in the present day.

The population of Brava, as in the other islands, quickly became more and more mixed. By the 1950s, the population in all islands was predominantly mestizo. The whites in Brava were in the minority.

As late as the 1950s, the religious schism that began when Martin Luther nailed *The 95 Theses* to the door of the Castle Church in Wittenberg, Germany, in 1517, still felt recent.[3] The minority white elite and the majority of the blacks and mestizos were Catholics, and the Catholicism was sanctioned by the state, even though freedom of religion had been proclaimed by the Portuguese Crown since 1910.

Capeverdeans who had immigrated to the United States, first in whaling ships, brought many things back to Brava, including a new religion—Protestantism. In the 1950s, the Protestants were in the minority. However, the building of a prominent Church of the Nazarene in the center of town—in the park—in the early 1900s was a portentous sign of things to come.

The Capeverdian culture was a culture born out of need—the need to depend on one another for survival. They were people contained in small islands surrounded by the immense sea and taking refuge inland among the rugged, volcanic mountains. With their backs against the mountains, the sea at their feet, and the blue sky above their heads, they found solidarity and comfort in their language, in their cuisine, in their music, and in their people, "*gente de terra.*" The Capeverdians learned to adapt, to respect, and to live with differences, and in spite of all the challenges, they became a generous people, and Brava especially became known as the land of hospitality, of "*morabesa.*"

"A Sweet Oblation" captures the spirit of this small community in the town of Villa de Nova Sintra, Brava, through the eyes of an eleven-year-old girl, herself facing change and asking the quintessential questions of why things are the way they are. The story takes place as the town, steeped in Catholic traditions and rituals, prepares itself for Easter. This simple story is, in essence, a study of the development of "self" in the nexus where life with its history, culture, play, ritual, religion, faith, family, duty, and yes, even bigotry, meet to elevate the soul into a higher state of understanding of what it means to be "human." But most importantly, it is a lesson in the sacredness of human relationship–key to the understanding of who we are and how we are related to each other in space and in time. It is in this nexus that lies the clues to the mystery of who we are and the answers to seminal questions of "Who am I, and what am I doing here?"

Chapter One
Carnival

Isabel Rodrigues and her two younger sisters, Ida and Mandy, and their live-in house helper, Maria, were spread out on the dining room floor, sorting out treats that they had collected from an afternoon of Carnival.

"Let's put all the fruit in one pile, the pieces of sugarcane on the other pile, and sweets over there, then we will divide them equally so that each one of us will get some of everything," Maria said in an attempt to prevent the Rodrigues sisters from fighting over who would get what, and also to ensure that she, herself, would get her fair share.

It had been a very hot afternoon in early March, the last day of the Carnival season.[4] The whole island was festive. The streets were decorated with bright, colorful banners. People of all ages moved in groups from street-to-street and from house-to-house, all dressed up in their favorite costumes—singing, dancing, and asking for some treats. Some people would even give live chickens, eggs, cassava, beans, and corn—everything that you would need to make a great "*merenda,*" the traditional meal for that evening.

There were also a lot of harmless practical jokes and drinking taking place. Regardless of who they were, everyone was at risk of being attacked by those who stayed home, sitting by their windows armed with rotten eggs, talcum powder, wheat flour, and buckets of ashes mixed with water, which they would throw over the heads of those who came by. Children were never the target of such pranks, but sometimes they found themselves in the path of a rotten egg or ashen water meant for someone else.

Isabel's group had been spared, having only been laced lightly by a cloud of talcum powder. They looked odd for a carnival group in Africa, but this was the expected norm for the Rodrigues children. They looked like they had just stepped out from New England in the late 1800s. Isabel was dressed as a Red Cross nurse, Ida was dressed up as an American Indian, Mandy was dressed up as a Salem witch, and Maria was dressed up as little Bo Peep. These costumes had been in the family for years and several generations of Rodrigues children had their pictures taken in them. The story went that their maternal great-grandfather, a captain on a whaling ship that sailed from the Cape Verde Islands to New Bedford, Massachusetts, in America, had brought the costumes home to Brava.

It was nearing five o'clock. It was still hot, and the girls were sweating under the old costumes. As they sorted the goodies, they nibbled on their favorites. Ida had a piece of sugarcane, Maria munched on a coconut sweet, and Mandy sucked on an orange. Mandy would have preferred a ripe *manginho,* a little mango of local variety, but it would not be in season until May.

She playfully pressed the orange with her little hands as she would have done with the *manginho* to liquefy the flesh inside as she chanted, "Little goat, little goat, give me some milk. Give me my sweet milk." She took a swig and then pressed on the fruit some more and chanted again, until the fruit went dry.

Isabel was not interested in anything on the piles. She was holding something tucked away against her chest, under the nurse's costume. She didn't know how long she could safely keep it there, so she feigned needing to go to the bathroom and disappeared among the trees in the backyard. She was back in no time, just as Maria was giving each girl, including herself, a piece from each pile of the goodies. She went round and round until there were only one or two pieces left in each pile, and when this happened, they bargained or traded for it.

Maria felt proud of herself having managed the situation without incident, unlike her past experience. Isabel quickly put her share in the lap of her skirt and went up the stairs. Everyone was contented with her share, and Carnival was ending on a happy note.

Chapter Two

Fern's Pranks and the Purple Cloths

As she was getting ready for bed that evening, Isabel could only think of the events of that afternoon. Her plan was to get up the next day very early before anyone else and go to the peach tree in the backyard. Although that had always been her hiding place, she never had hidden anything so precious and perishable as this before. Isabel's face was flushed and her heart raced. She could hardly wait for dawn to come.

Isabel glanced over at the bed that she shared with Ida and saw that she was already fast asleep, tuckered out from the day's activities. Mandy was also sleeping soundly on her little bed in the corner of the room.

It was a fitting end to the Carnival season. Fern will be proud of me when she learns about this, she thought. Her mouth watered, and she glossed her lips repeatedly with the tip of her tongue.

Isabel was already feeling nostalgic about this Carnival season. Fern, one of Isabel's older sisters, always made the season fun. Isabel giggled as she thought of all the pranks and practical jokes that Fern had pulled in town that year. Isabel couldn't help herself. She covered her mouth with her hands to muffle her laugher so as not to awaken Ida. She thought of how Fern methodically captured all of *Nhõ* Tutu's pigeons. *Nhõ* Tutu was one of the island's elders and distinguished gentlemen who lived on the next street over from the Rodrigues.' He was a widower and lived by himself. He was proud of his flock of pigeons. The flock was well known throughout the island, and like clockwork, he would let them out of their coops from the widow's walk of his house at about seven o'clock in the morning. The pigeons would fly over the Rodrigues' house and disappear over the mountains. No one knew where they went, but by sunset the flock would reappear over the mountains, fly again over the Rodrigues' house, and *Nhõ* Tutu would be there at the widow's walk to welcome them and to tuck them in their coops for the night. *Nhõ* Tutu took pride in these pigeons as if they were his own children.

"I wonder what would happen if one day *Nhõ* Tutu's pigeons didn't come home?" Fern mischievously asked Isabel one day. Fern was pretty tight-lipped, but once in a while she let Isabel in on her plans. She devised a plan that would answer her own question, and Carnival was the perfect time. Practical jokes were accepted and encouraged during Carnival season, as long as they were done in fun and no one was harmed.[5] Her plan was to trap every single one of *Nhõ* Tutu's pigeons, slowly, in a manner that would not immediately cause suspicion.

Her trap was simple. She got an old bamboo basket that her mother used to carry crops from the field. She propped the basket up with a stick that was tied to a long string. Under the basket, she put plenty of ground up yellow corn. She placed the trap on the roof of the barn, which was directly below the pigeons' flight path. Every morning and evening, she sat at the window with a clear view of the roof of the barn, holding on to the end of the string, on the lookout for the pigeons. Isabel sometimes joined her on this vigil. Soon enough the pigeons became aware of the bright yellow corn on the roof of the barn, and as soon as the pigeons were safely under the basket, Fern would pull on the string and the pigeons would be trapped. Every day she caught two or three pigeons this way. There was a small alcove across from the barn that was not usually in use, and that became the captured pigeons' new home. Fern took good care of her captives giving them plenty of food and water.

After three days and ten pigeons short, *Nhõ* Tutu was seen in the park, the main public square, in front of the Rodrigues' house looking quite distraught. Fern had all his pigeons in captivity within two weeks. No one knew what had happened to the pigeons. *Nhõ* Tutu even approached Mr. Rodrigues with his dilemma. Mr. Rodrigues confronted Fern because he suspected that the pigeon heist had his daughter's signature all over it. Fern admitted nothing, but immediately began to release the pigeons in the same slow and deliberate manner in which she had captured them. Isabel and Fern were deeply moved by *Nhõ* Tutu's jubilation when his pigeons began to reappear, one by one. Two days before Carnival, *Nhõ* Tutu had his entire flock back.

As Isabel was later to find out, the capture of *Nhõ* Tutu's pigeons was not the only thing in Fern's repertoire of pranks. One Carnival Sunday afternoon,

Fern decided to steal *Nhã* Oliva's family supper right from under her nose. *Nhã* Oliva was a cousin of Mrs. Rodrigues, and the families were very close. They lived down the avenue from the Rodrigues.' *Nhã* Oliva loved to spend part of her Sunday afternoon by the wall barrier that separated her house from the avenue. Usually she met other ladies there and they chatted, entertained by the comings and goings of people passing by. She usually left supper, warm and ready, by the stove. Fern knew this from spending so much time in her house. So Fern waited until the ladies were deep into their conversations, and then she snuck around through *Nhã* Oliva's front door, stole the pots with food, took them home through the backyard, and hid them in the kitchen. Fern then kept watch for the ladies until each went their own way home. No sooner did *Nhã* Oliva disappear into her house then she came back outside, yelling out, loud in desperation,

"*Nhã djantá! Nhã djantá*! (My supper! My supper!) Someone has stolen my family's supper," as she ran towards the Rodrigues' house. Meanwhile, Fern slipped out through the back door and put the pots back exactly as she had found them. She was back in a flash, just in time to participate in the commotion about who would stoop so low as to steal a family's supper. Fern also made sure that she was part of the entourage accompanying *Nhã* Oliva back to her house to witness the dismay in her face when she found the pots exactly where she first had left them.

But of all of Fern's pranks, the one that Isabel loved the most (and she began to laugh uncontrollably as she was remembering it) was the case of Gustavo and the corn bread. Every night Mrs. Rodrigues would make a *gufongo*, a type of corn bread, for the next day's breakfast. She would shape it into a loaf and then wrap it with green banana leaves. She then would clear the hot ashes and charcoal from the wooden stove and would set the *gufongo* on the hot brick and cover it with the hot ashes. She usually would do this by seven o'clock in the evening and the *gufongo* would be baked and ready to be taken out three hours later. Taking the *gufongo* out and storing it for the next day's breakfast was the sacred job of Gustavo. Gustavo was a longtime, live-in herdsman who worked for the Rodrigues family. He had his room next to the kitchen. He was extremely fond of Mrs. Rodrigues and took that special job of taking the *gufongo* out on time very seriously. Fern thought that he was even a bit fanatical about it. It didn't matter where he was; he made sure that he was back in time to take out the *gufongo*.

So Fern saw this as a perfect opportunity to pull a fast one on Gustavo. She got a piece of stone, roughly the shape of the *gufongo*, and softened its edges with clay. She took care to mold it until it looked and felt just like the real bread. She then wrapped it in banana leaves exactly as her mother would have done and replaced the *gufongo* with the stone one. She kept a vigil for Gustavo. As soon as she saw him coming out of his room she called her sisters to come and look. Well, Gustavo took the corn bread out and tried to press into it for doneness as he usually did, but this time the corn bread would not spring back. He loosened half of the burnt banana leaves and blew the ashes away. He kept flipping that *gufongo* every which way and cried out in desperation,

"Oh, Mrs. Rodrigues is going to kill me. This *gufongo* is burnt through and through! It is as hard as a rock!" As he said that, all the kids broke out into a roaring laugher. A startled Gustavo almost dropped the stone *gufongo* on his foot.

Fern immediately walked over to him with the real corn bread and said with a grin, "Don't worry,

Gustavo. Here is your *gufongo*. It is perfect. The one you are holding is indeed a rock." The kids couldn't help themselves and doubled over with laugher. Gustavo and Mrs. Rodrigues didn't think it was funny, but it was Carnival season, and they should have known better with Fern around.

Isabel was bursting in laughter, remembering those pranks, when Mrs. Rodrigues walked in to her room.

"What is so funny?" she asked.

"Oh, I was just thinking about all the pranks that Fern has pulled this Carnival. I am going to miss Carnival," she added.

"Well, I must admit, Fern outdid herself this time around," Mrs. Rodrigues said, shaking her head and suppressing a smile, "but the fun is over. We now have to turn our minds to more serious matters." As she said this, she took a purple cloth from a stack of cloths that she had brought in with her and proceeded to drape the small brass crucifix that hung over Isabel's bed. Then she added, "Tomorrow is Ash Wednesday, the beginning of Lent."

Isabel frowned.

"You are now old enough to begin to follow

some of the Church's rules for Lent," her mother said as she faced Isabel.

"What church rules?" Isabel asked.

"A time to fast, pray, do penance, and give alms," her mother answered simply.

"What?!" Isabel screamed out incredulously.

"Hush, don't wake up your sisters. Tomorrow we will talk about this. I am glad that you had a lot of fun and sweets today," her mother said, her lips slightly puckered, her eyes squinted as if trying to focus, nodding her head slightly as she left the room carrying with her the rest of the purple cloths.

Isabel sat at the foot of her bed, her head tilted downwards, and her mouth slightly open with her fingers touching her exposed front teeth.

Isabel thought, *Mother couldn't have known! How could she know? But Mother has her ways of knowing things.* She thought about sneaking out to the peach tree and taking care of it right then and there, but it was already dark and someone was bound to miss her or even spot her.

I will sneak out at the first light tomorrow—Ash Wednesday or no Ash Wednesday. Besides, who is going to know? she thought with resolve.

So with these thoughts in mind, Isabel knelt

by her bed, blessed herself, folded her hands, and looked up towards the crucifix to say her prayer, but there was no crucifix. There was only a blob of purple cloth. She closed her eyes and said her prayer, and suddenly she was taken over by a feeling of emptiness that she had never known before. For the first time in her life, she wondered if there was anyone really up there listening. She shivered and climbed into bed, snuggling tight against Ida's warm little body.

She lay in her bed unable to find a comfortable position to sleep. She spent the whole night half-asleep and half-awake. Her thoughts were all jumbled up between her plan to sneak out early and her fear that her mother would catch her in the act. Her mother's words, "A time to fast, pray, do penance, and give alms," kept echoing in her head. She cried out, "No! No!" She woke up in a sweat and sat up. Her heart felt like the pump in the cistern of her aunt's house when someone was vigorously drawing out water. She cuddled up closely to Ida and finally dozed off again.

Chapter Three

The Secret

Isabel woke up and sat up on her bed with the first crow of the old rooster. She looked out the window. It was still dark, but the red glow of the rising sun in the east silhouetted the tall papaya trees that flanked the house near her bedroom. She took a deep breath. For despite the frantic night, she was determined to follow through with her plans. She waited until there was enough light for her to see the interior of the house. She did not want to be stumbling about and waking anyone up. She quickly dressed and tiptoed out of her room in her bare feet. She took small, light steps. Even so, the old bare hardwood floors creaked. She took several steps and then stopped. Several more careful light steps, and she again stopped and listened. The creaking floor did not awaken anyone. It was the normal noise in their house, she decided. She was paying such close attention to where she was stepping that she did not notice the row of purple blobs that hung all along the hallway wall.

It wasn't until she was going down the stairs and facing the front door that she noticed something amiss. Behind the front door, her parents kept a special picture of Jesus with His chest open, His sacred heart exposed with a crown of thorns around it.[6] In that picture, Jesus had a warm, loving, compassionate look, and He gazed straight out. His right hand was giving a blessing, and His left hand was pointing to His heart. The wound in His left hand was clearly visible. Isabel had often been intrigued by this picture and had asked her mother about it. She had told her that the picture was there to bless and protect their family and also to bless anyone who stepped inside their house. The picture was only noticeable when the front door was closed and you were descending the staircase as Isabel was now doing. Isabel was halfway down the stairs when she noticed that the picture was no longer there. There was only the blob of purple cloth. The feeling of emptiness that had engulfed her just the night before came back. She shivered and held on tightly to her stomach.

Once outside, the cool, damp air choked her. She took several shallow breaths. Fog hung over the mountains. No one was up yet, not even Gustavo, who was usually the first one up to tend to the animals. The old rooster was crowing intermittently, and it was now being joined by several others. She looked towards the east, and the sky was being painted with long, narrow strokes of color gently chasing away the darkness. She could see the outline of the neighboring island of Fogo and its volcanic peak shrouded by heavy, dark clouds. She wondered if this was how it was every dawn. It looked and felt like a different world, barely resembling her everyday surroundings. As she reached the gate that led to the backyard, her destination became clear. She ran to the peach tree. The box was wet. She opened it and there it was-her treasure-snuggled under the damp newspaper. Trembling, she picked it up. She stopped and looked about, and then she took off the newspaper. She brought it up to her nose and smelled it as if it were a delicate flower. She closed her eyes and breathed in the aroma. She then carefully loosened the gold paper wrapping and took another whiff. She held her breath.

If someone were watching, they would have

thought that Isabel was in deep prayer and making an offering to the gods. Crouched down on her knees, she was wearing a light pink calico dress, which blended with the rose colors of the dawn, her long black hair draped over her pale bare shoulders with bangs framing her round face. Her eyes were closed, and her head was uplifted towards the rising sun. Her hands, with joined palms open, held the offering.

Isabel loosened the corner of the inner gold wrapper. Her heart fluttered. She brought her nose very close, almost touching the dark delicacy. She extended the tip of her tongue and was about to taste it, but she hesitated. Something kept her from permitting her tongue even to touch the dark surface. She thought that she heard something. She looked around, but there was no one. *But soon someone will be out here*, she thought. The roosters were now reaching their crescendo. It seemed that every rooster in the island was crowing in unison. *How can anyone sleep through this*? Isabel wondered. But this was the normal rhythm of the dawn, and she could not remember ever hearing or seeing it like this before. Alarmed that someone might be coming she quickly rewrapped everything, replaced it in the box, and put it deep into the hollow root of the tree. She stopped the hole with stones and camouflaged it with leaves. She quickly returned to her bed unseen.

Isabel lay in her bed—still. Both her hands clutched her chest as she tried to calm the storm that had taken over her heart. Her dress was damp. She shivered and her teeth chattered uncontrollably. She then brought the corner of her blanket up to her chin and held it there with both hands. She was dazzled by the experience of the dawn, and she felt haunted by her secret. She lay there hardly breathing and stared through the window as the sunlight slowly brought back the forms of her familiar surroundings. After a while, she heard Gustavo, Maria, and others in the courtyard and knew that Lent was upon her. She fell into a deep sleep, lulled by the rhythmic thud of the women pounding corn at a distance.

Chapter Four
Ash Wednesday

There was no school on Ash Wednesday, so Isabel and her sisters stayed in bed much later than usual, but even so, they were all dressed and seated at the breakfast table by nine o'clock. This was going to be a day of fasting for all adults in the house and children twelve years and older. Although Isabel was not technically of age yet, her twelfth birthday would fall right in the middle of Holy Week. Isabel was supposed to fast like everybody else; her mother had informed her that morning.[7] That meant drinking only water and nothing else during the day; however, there would be a *caldo de pexe* (a fish stew, mostly broth) in the evening.

"Isabel, you can be excused from the table. Go and see if your sisters Eliza and Fern need help with anything. I will see that Ida and Mandy have their breakfast," Mrs. Rodrigues said firmly trying to avoid a confrontation.

Isabel stood up immediately from the table, quickly took two steps towards the door, and then stopped and turned around to face her mother. Her mother, who was in no mood for Isabel's antics, looked back intently at her with her eyes wide open, her right arm out, and her extended index finger pointed Isabel towards the door. Isabel opened her mouth to say something, but only a pathetic shrieking noise of protest came out. She was angry; after all, she was not yet twelve. She had six more weeks of being eleven years old and her mother was being unfair. She was not through with being eleven yet. She had important things to do before she turned twelve, and one of them was waiting, hidden in the hollowed root of the peach tree. She was convinced that involving her in this whole Lenten ritual was her mother's way of teaching her a lesson. She probably knew about her secret. *If anyone would know if Mother knew anything, it would be Fern. Fern seems to be always one step ahead of everybody else in knowing what is going on in the house*, Isabel thought, but efforts to get any information from Fern proved futile.

Under different circumstances, Isabel

wouldn't have minded the fasting. She would even have considered it an honor—being elevated to the ranks of "fasting" adults. She was tired of always being lumped together with her two younger sisters. Fasting for Lent would signal to the whole world that she was no longer a "baby." She even imagined a beautiful angel blowing a trumpet announcing it in Heaven, "Isabel Rodrigues is now a fasting member of the human race!" All the angels would clap, and she would take a big bow before the Father, on His throne. Then one of the angels would take her hand and help her step up onto a platform next to her older siblings and her parents, while she would look down at Ida and Mandy—*the babies*!

Although the thought of her new status on earth, perhaps even in Heaven, thrilled her, she was troubled and was becoming even a bit defiant and bitter. She kept asking herself, *Why fast? What is the big deal about fasting anyway*? It didn't make a bit of sense to her, except that her mother was being plain mean and made the excuse that she was coming of age. She reasoned, *Why didn't Mother think of me coming of age yesterday and let me participate in the Carnival festivities with Fern and Eliza? No, that would have been too much fun for Isabel. She remembered Isabel coming of age only when it came time to suffer! Yes, that is it. Mother must have seen me in the backyard and decided that she was going to teach me a lesson! Mother makes me so mad.* At that, Isabel stopped and jumped up and down with both of her fists clenched. She paced up and down in the courtyard thinking, *Just because mother thinks that her life hasn't been so hot she now wants to put the screws on Isabel. That is it! Just when she saw that I had gotten something and kept it all to myself, she came up with this Lent story. Maybe Nhõ Americano meant it for me to share it with the others, or maybe not. It wasn't as if he gave it to me and said, 'share this with your group.' No, he never said anything like that. In fact, he carefully put it in the palm of my hand and wrapped my fingers around it without the others noticing. I didn't ask for it. I had not even dreamed about it. By chance it fell right in my lap.* She decided that she must confront her mother and the sooner the better.

So Isabel sat on the stone steps that led from the main house into the courtyard and to the kitchen and waited for her mother. It was only ten o'clock, but it was already very hot. Isabel was grateful that the backyard was shady and cool, but still she was worried that her hidden treasure might melt. She would not let her mother with her Lenten rituals deprive her of her pleasure. Periodically, she peeked into the breakfast room. *Mother is taking her time today*, she thought. At last, her mother came out and Isabel jumped to her feet and blurted out, "Can I help you with those dishes, Mother?"

"Oh! Isabel," her mother replied balancing the dishes so they wouldn't fall down on the cobbled stone. "No, it's okay. Since Ida and Mandy are the only ones eating today, there is not much to do," she added.

"I guess that is one good thing about Ash Wednesday," Isabel responded rather sarcastically.

"What do you mean?" her mother replied.

"Oh, I was just thinking," Isabel explained as she walked a few steps ahead of her mother, while turning around and walking sideways so as to face her. "Compared to yesterday, this house, this town, and this whole island appears dead. No eating, no drinking, no singing, no dancing, and practically everybody is wearing dark clothes. The sun is shining as usual and the sky is as blue as usual, but everything feels so different, so sad and so empty."

Mrs. Rodrigues quickly stopped and looked

down at Isabel, surprised by her young daughter's demeanor and words. She was used to her drama, but there was a passion on her daughter's voice that she had not heard before. She said, "That is the whole point of Lent!" She continued to walk across the courtyard towards the kitchen with the few dirty cups and saucers from the breakfast.

"That is exactly what I wanted to ask you," Isabel replied, following her mother to the kitchen, "What is the point of Lent? What is the point of fasting? What is the point of draping all the religious pictures in our house with those purple cloths?"

Mrs. Rodrigues absentmindedly rested the dishes on a little three-legged table that was anchored to the back corner of the wall of the kitchen. Her mind was processing Isabel's questions and was searching for answers. She sat on the stone stool by the corn grinder. Isabel sat on the other stool across from her. The stone grinder sat idle between them.

Normally, the kitchen would be teeming with activity, but today it was empty, quiet, and eerie. There were no three-legged, cast iron black cauldrons on the stove with lunch being prepared—the ashes lay cold. There was no smoke coming out from the chimney; the woodbin under the stove was empty with but a few straggling pieces of kindling left over from the night before. The big stone *pilon* (pestle), usually surrounded by women pounding corn to prepare for supper, was turned upside down on the ground, and several wooden mortars rested behind it against a corner of the wall by the kitchen entrance. A tall, clay pot with water from the cistern rested in the back corner opposite the table.

It was a small, functional kitchen built entirely of stone. One side was built up from the ground into a platform where stones were set up as a tripod to hold up the three-legged cast iron pots of different sizes, leaving a space under them where wood was placed and the fire lit. A huge chimney rose up from the stove. Sometimes strings of *linguiça* (sausages) would be strung there to smoke. The walls were all of stone, unfinished, with cracks used for storage. Mrs. Rodrigues often hid a few cents for a rainy day by the wall next to the stone grinder where she now sat. Gustavo stored his tobacco and the small bamboo mortar and pestle that he used to grind his roasted tobacco, and Maria kept matches, salt, and spices wrapped in brown paper. Years of soot and smoke had blackened the four walls and the ceiling. The stone floor, polished from constant use, hid under some firewood residue.

There were no windows; there was only the one door leading to the courtyard and to the main house.

In spite of the soot and the smoke, the aroma from the Crioulo cooking and the warmth of the fire made this kitchen a cozy, comforting place. At dusk a small oil lamp lit the table area where Gustavo sat on the wooden bench to eat his supper and smoke his pipe. Isabel and her little sisters loved to sit on his lap, dazzled by the glow of the firelight, enchanted by the aroma of his tobacco, and riveted by his many stories about people in strange lands. It was here, oddly enough, where the many dramas of the Rodrigues household often played out.

Although the sun was bright outside, the kitchen itself was lit only partially by the rays of the sun that penetrated through the small door. Isabel's back was towards the courtyard; she faced the dark interior and her mother. Mrs. Rodrigues, sitting across from Isabel, was facing the courtyard. The sunlight lit her face and exposed the furrows in her brow. Her face was thoughtful. Her hands were folded, covering her mouth. Her eyes were lowered, looking down at the grinder as if she were asking it for the answers. It was here while spending many hours grinding the corn that she herself had pondered these same questions as Isabel's. She paused, and her lips quivered, trying to form words that her eleven-year-old daughter could understand. She mentally asked for divine guidance. It was the first time that she would be articulating aloud what she had been pondering for years.

Chapter Five

Mina

Mrs. Rodrigues gently smiled at Isabel, bent over the grinder, and touched her hands lightly. Isabel's face was shadowed, but her mother felt her anxiety and the tension in her body.

"I am going to tell you a story," her mother finally said. Isabel sat attentively holding onto the handle of the grinder.

"Once upon a time . . . ," her mother began. She stopped and took in a deep breath. Then she began again, "Once upon a time, there lived a little girl named Mina. Mina lived in the land of Djeu. It is said that her ancestors arrived from far away lands in ships long ago. No one in Djeu knew exactly from where they came, but soon they proved to be very hardworking and pleasant. The people of Djeu accepted them as their own. Mina never thought much about her ancestors and would have been very happy to be just like anyone else in Djeu. But the people from Djeu were dark and olive-skinned, with dark hair and eyes. Mina had light skin, with yellow hair and blue eyes. It seemed that every time that Mina went out, people would comment on her long yellow hair that looked like the lustrous strands of silk from a young ear of corn. They marveled at her eyes, which they said were blue and sparkling like the sea that surrounded them, and her skin was soft and reminded them of the rich cream that they used to make their finest butter.

"Mina often wished to be like her older sister, Mana, who was in many ways like the Djeu people. She was gregarious, had many friends, and delighted in gossiping, and she enjoyed the many diversions that she and her youthful friends would engage in. Mina felt estranged from everyone. She was quiet, pensive, and somber. She had few friends. Mana's flirtations bored her.

"An unfortunate thing happened—both of their parents died young. Mina took responsibility for her household when she was only nine years old, under the guidance of her grandmother. Her grandmother was an astute and intelligent woman, and she loved her granddaughters very much. She was particularly fond of Mina. Mina learned everything that her grandmother could teach her. She thought her grandmother was very wise and perhaps that she would help her understand herself. Mana could not understand her and had little patience with Mina's brooding, especially given Mina's coveted exotic beauty."

Mrs. Rodrigues stopped and stared for a few seconds at her rough calloused hands and continued, "Indeed, as Mina grew up she became more and more beautiful, but with all that beauty, she also became more and more somber and disciplined. Towards Mana, she acted more like a mother than a younger sister. So it was no surprise that young men from the land of Djeu became enchanted with Mina. But Mina, to the chagrin of her sister and grandmother, found no joy in this.

" 'Marry, you must!' her old grandmother counseled her rather forcefully. Her grandmother was getting old, and both girls needed to secure good husbands. Mina could have had the pick of the best young men in all Djeu, but there was no joy in Mina's heart, and none of the young men were able to stir any passion in her.

"When Mina married, she accepted her grandmother's choice. Of her marriage, she confessed to Mana that she felt like a young bird shot and wounded while attempting its first flight. Such sentiments were beyond Mana's comprehension, and for that matter, beyond most people in Djeu.

Mina had many children, but she did not delight in them, and her husband was lost as to what would make her happy.

"One summer afternoon, Mina sat alone by the bed, breastfeeding her youngest. She looked down at the baby vigorously sucking away at her breast with his eyes closed and beads of sweat dotting his face. Mina felt tired. She leaned back on the chair and took a deep breath. She closed her eyes and muttered, 'How many years of my life have I spent with a baby at my breast?' It seemed to her that most of her life, people, including her own children, had been taking something from her and giving her nothing back. She began to think of her grandmother, and for an instant, she felt loved, but grandmother had been dead for over ten years. Mina's body ached, her hair had lost its luster, and she had lost almost all of her teeth. 'When will all this end?' she cried out in pain to her grandmother. She began to cry uncontrollably. She felt like she was a strange beast in the land of Djeu. She screamed out, 'I am here just to suffer, to work. I am little better than the donkey that carries the manure on its back to the fields.' Her scream alarmed the baby, and the baby began to cry.

" 'Oh! I am sorry.' Mina got up and began to pace back and forth, trying to quiet the baby in between her sobs. Then Mina stopped her whimpering. She was standing right in front of a crucifix that hung by the side of her bed.

"Mina stared at the crucifix for the longest time. The crucifix had always been there, but Mina had paid little attention to it. Religion and prayer were prominent features of the daily life of the Djeudians, but even in this, Mina also differed from them. Her stare took her beyond the metal and beyond the wood of the cross."

Isabel, who up to this point had sat quietly, riveted by her mother's story, got up, and in agitation asked, "What did she see? What did she see, Mother?"

"People say that Mina was transformed-that Christ, on the cross, perhaps spoke to her," her mother continued. "Some people say that Mina's cry joined the cry of Christ on the cross. To be certain,

Mina saw her suffering in the body of Christ crucified. She was made to understand that her suffering
was a blessing."[8]

"A blessing?" Isabel tilted her head and gave
her mother a quizzical look.

"People say that Mina was reminded of how
kind Jesus was even when He was on the cross.
He comforted and consoled people. He gave them
encouragement and hope even when He was in the
most excruciating pain. People say that Mina, by
some miracle, understood in her heart the reason for
Jesus' suffering and also for her own."

"What was that?" Isabel quickly asked.

"What was what?" her mother responded
confused by the interruption in her train of thought.

"The reason why Jesus had to suffer?" Isabel
clarified.

Her mother continued, "Because, through the
suffering, Jesus was reunited with His Father, and we,
through Jesus, get reunited with God at the cross."

Isabel sat down again, squinted, wiped her
brow, and was about to say something but decided
not to. Her mother bent her head to the side and gestured to her as if to say, "Do you want to ask something?" Isabel shook her head.

So her mother continued, "God gives us tribu-
lation–suffering–so that we can get close to Him and
become like Him. We are God's children, but we forget it. God has to keep reminding us that we belong
to Him and that this is not our home. Our true home
is up there." Her mother raised her gaze upwards and
pointed towards the sky. "We always seek pleasure
from the outside, and that is fine, to a certain extent.
Like yesterday, our whole neighborhood was happy–
lots of eating, drinking, dancing, and playing jokes
on each other. If we are always happy, if we always
have everything we want, we may fall into the temp-
tation of feeling that we can go at it alone, that we are
the masters of our destinies, and that we don't need
God–that this is our home. God loves us too much to
let us go on thinking like that."

Isabel looked like a beautifully blown bal-
loon that had lost considerable air.

"I don't understand, Mother," she said sound-
ing a bit discouraged.

Her mother continued, "Okay, you like to
go play at your friend Dee's house. You like all her
toys, her dolls, and her beautiful bicycle. Sometimes,
when you are riding her bicycle and having all the
fun, I call you to come home, right?"

Isabel nodded, and added, "And you always seem to do it right when I am having the most fun too!"

"Well, it may seem that way, but what if I never called you? What if we forgot all about you and left you there?"

"I would miss you, Mandy, Ida, and everybody. I would miss my bed, my doll and . . ."

"You see, Isabel. This is how it is with God. Many times He stops our fun, and sometimes He even has to drag us by our ears so that we can come home."

"Wow!" Isabel said.

"And this, my dear Isabel, is what Lent is all about-removing ourselves from the things that give us temporary pleasure in order to seek the joy that is spiritual and everlasting. So to answer your questions, this is the why of Lent, the why of fasting, and also the why of almsgiving."

"But, but I still don't understand why Mina, the most beautiful girl that had ever lived in Djeu, was so miserable and unhappy? It doesn't make sense," she said as she let a burst of air escape noisily from her puckered lips.

Mrs. Rodrigues did not answer for a while.

She looked down, then up, and held her gaze on the ceiling for a few minutes. Then she began, "Well, Isabel, this is very complicated—why Mina, in spite of her great beauty, was so miserable, I really don't know. But people say that Mina's beautiful body had taken over her spirit." Mrs. Rodrigues paused and then continued, "We are great spirits, created by God to be like Him. But as you remember in the story of Adam and Eve, something happened." Before Mrs. Rodrigues could continue, Isabel jumped up and down on her seat, raised her right index finger up in the air as she was accustomed to do in school when she knew the answer, and blurted out, "Oh! Oh! I know. I know what happened! They ate the apple that God had told them not too."

Mrs. Rodrigues smiled and said, "That is correct, Isabel, but the eating of the forbidden apple may have been a simple way of telling us that something terrible happened-something so terrible that the light of God, our own spirit, was all but snuffed out of us. So that the body began to pretend that it was God."

"I don't understand," Isabel responded, rather distraught.

"Let's see." Her mother paused and looked around, searching for an idea of how better to explain to Isabel. She nodded her head in delight, and asked, "We have this beautiful house, right?"

Isabel nodded her head and said, "Right!"

"We are the most important thing in this house. Our ancestors built this house for us—to give us shelter, for us to invite our friends, for us to put our treasures, for our pictures, to eat our meals, to sleep, and all the other good stuff. What if, by some unthinkable event-a mysterious wind from the east whispered something to the house and put in the house's mind that IT could be the master, and the house managed by some unthinkable event, to make us all prisoners and lock us down under the boards where you and your sisters go hunting for old coins. Instead of us being the master of our house, our house acted like it was the master. How do you think we would be feeling under the wooden boards?" her mother finally asked.

"We would not be happy down there. There is only dirt down there. There are spiders and rats too. We would be coughing a lot. We would not be able to stand up, and we would be crawling on our bellies all the time. We would eat dirt, and it is always dark," Isabel responded, recalling her last experience on a treasure hunt under the wooden floors with her sisters.

"Yes," her mother answered, and there was a long pause. Then she added, "The house would look as beautiful as it did before, but it would be miserable. Who would come in when there was all that misery going on under those wooden boards?"

Isabel was mesmerized and couldn't make a sound.

"People say that Mina, at that moment when she faced the cross, understood the vastness of her being. She understood that she was much more than her body. She was filled with joy and God's love, and she began to see her babies and everything around her as a blessing and joy. At the moment, we can say that one of the boards was yanked opened and her spirit escaped and began to be master again."

"So what happened to Mina afterwards?' Isabel pursued.

"Her life continued as usual, but she understood that her 'differentness' was a gift from God and that any suffering that might have resulted from it was a way to keep her close to God."

Isabel frowned and asked, "How is that?"

"Like I said, Isabel, if we want to get our spirit

aligned with the Spirit of God, if we want to find our way home to our Father and Creator, we have to follow Jesus' example. Suffering of whatever degree or source is a tool that will take us there. At least, this is my understanding. When you grow up, you may arrive at your own understanding, and that will be between you and God."

"So Mina had a happy life afterwards?" Isabel asked.

"Yes. People say that she lived to a ripe, old age, and she did many good things for people, even traveling outside Djeu. Her many children, grandchildren, and great-grandchildren cherished her very much, and her husband loved her and was dedicated to her. The legend goes that during her last days, she was very sick and kept her eyes closed all the time, but the day that she died she opened her eyes, and many people gathered to look at her beautiful, sparkling blue eyes. The Djeudians have never again seen anyone like Mina. People believe that she is a great saint in Heaven." Mrs. Rodrigues smiled at her daughter.

Isabel sat quietly taken in by her mother's story, and when she came to, she asked, "What about the purple cloths? Why do you have to cover every saint's picture and every cross all over the house?"

"The pictures remind us of God and the goodness of God. The fast is not only for the belly but also for the eyes. When we don't see any symbol of God, we long for Him, and we are forced to go deeper into our souls in search of Him."

Isabel nodded her head but said nothing. She wanted to tell her mother how she had felt the night before and early that morning when she only saw the purple blobs, but she decided to say nothing—lest she get caught and have to reveal all to her mother at that moment.

Chapter Six
Church

"Isabel! Isabel! You need to get ready for church!" Eliza, her older sister, yelled out from the back veranda on the second floor of the house that overlooked the courtyard. Isabel and her mother were still sitting by the corn grinder in the kitchen, each deep in her own thoughts.

"Do I have to?" Isabel asked her mother.

"Yes, you do!" her mother replied emphatically.

In other times, she would have argued and would have pointed out that her mother hardly ever went to church herself. It was not fair for her to make them go, but at that moment, she was feeling differently. The story of Mina had a strange effect on her. She felt introspective, and the anger and gloom that she had felt earlier had all but dissipated.

"I will bring you some ashes," Isabel told her mother cheerfully. Her mother did not respond. Mrs. Rodrigues was already at the stove blowing on some coals to heat the iron so that she could touch up the girls' dresses and her husband's shirt for church.

Isabel liked going to church most of the time, but sometimes church scared her[9]. It seemed haunted with all the statues of the saints dressed in long robes with their heads covered, some with wounds oozing streams of blood, which glistened in the light from the rows upon rows of lit candles. Isabel often would observe people feverishly fingering their rosaries in front of the statues and would wonder about the dreadful problems that they had that they were asking the saints for help.

Of all the saints' statues in the church, Isabel had a personal issue with Saint John the Baptist, their patron saint. People of his time thought that he was a lunatic, and Isabel thought that he looked the part too. And what they said he ate was purely disgusting to Isabel–locusts and wild honey. Locust, she was later to find out, was a fancy name for plain grasshopper. Yuck! What Isabel thought was even stranger about Saint John the Baptist was that young Catholic women could pray to him for help in finding husbands. *What did he know about romance anyways?* Isabel wondered. From what she had heard about his life, he could have cared less about the fancies of young people's hearts. Nevertheless, he had a very strong following among the young people of the island.

On Sundays, church wasn't too bad. It was always full of people and was well lit, with fresh bouquets of flowers on the altar. On weekdays, church was a forbidden territory. You went there only on a dare from your friends. One day Isabel had gone by herself on a weekday. In Sunday school, she had heard a story about a little girl who was now a great saint in Heaven. This little girl had loved Jesus so much that she often went to visit Him in her church. Isabel was so moved by this story that she had decided that she, too, was going to follow this little girl's example and visit Jesus in her own church.

One day after school, she quietly slipped out and went to church. The church was dark, and she didn't think that anyone was there. Isabel could see the little red light up in the altar that told her that Jesus was there in the consecrated host, waiting for her. She did not dare to go all the way in, so she knelt, barely inside the doorway, on the floor. As it happened, there was a priest decorating the altar for the upcoming holiday. Seeing Isabel, he stood up and bellowed out some words that she did not understand. He gestured for her to get out, just as her mother had done to her at home that morning. Isabel had gotten out and had run all the way home. That priest had reminded her of John the Baptist. She imagined him yelling with honey dripping from the corner of his mouth and exposing locust wings stuck between his teeth, "Get out of here! Don't bother me! I have better things to do." Isabel had never been this scared in her whole life. The priest had thought that she was just a nosy kid, whereas Isabel had been try-ing to imitate a saint. *How stupid*! Isabel would scold herself whenever she remembered the episode, and she would flush with embarrassment. That was two years ago, and she had never again stepped inside the church unless it was on Sunday for Mass or for Sunday school. The story of that little girl, however, had never left her.

On Sundays, she felt safe going to church. People and priests were all on their best behavior, trying to get favors from God, and many times they were too scared to ask God directly. They felt as if they had to ask Jesus' mother or one of the saints to ask for them. Isabel thought that this was a good system, and it worked well even within her own family. Once there was a picnic sponsored by her school. She wanted to go, so she whispered it to Fern, who whispered it to Eliza, who whispered it to her mother, who in turn whispered it to her father, and soon her mother was packing her a picnic lunch to take. Sometimes it did not work that way. It depended on how her relationship was with God or her father at a given time. Often she felt confident enough to go straight to God and ask, but her own father was a different story. She was grateful that there were other ways, no less effective routes, to get what you wanted. Isabel had become a student of this and had tried these methods to get things from her teacher, her family, and her friends.

As she was getting older, things were getting more complicated, and this new twist that her mother had just thrown in with Lent was confusing her. Her mother's story, instead of clarifying things, confused her even more. "Suffering is a way to God." Isabel kept pondering these words from her mother.

Indeed, suffering was all around her. As long as she could remember, she had always been told that suffering was a bad, but necessary, thing that you had to go through to get to God. All the saints in her church had suffered one way or another, even Jesus. *God did not even spare Him from suffering, so it has to be extremely important*, Isabel thought. It did not make any sense to her, and she had yet to find anyone who understood it completely.

She knew many people who were suffering from all kinds of illnesses and misfortune with no one to turn to but the Church. Isabel knew that her family was not poor. Her family was practically one of the founding families of their community. They had property, a good house, and were members of the upper class. Isabel's family, like all the other families who depended on agriculture for their livelihoods, had become impoverished from years of drought and repeated crop failures. Yet her family had always managed and was able to provide her and her siblings with the basics. Isabel herself had very little experience with suffering, although she had developed a tendency to romanticize the suffering of others, especially that of the saints whom she was always hearing about in Sunday school.

Eliza helped her get dressed for Ash Wednesday Mass. "The Mass begins at home as you prepare to go to church," she had been told. Going to Mass was a solemn thing, and you had to prepare yourself by looking your very best. Today Isabel wore a navy blue cotton dress with little white flowers, which her mother had made for Eliza several years ago when Eliza's godmother died. She wore white shoes freshly polished, with white socks, and instead of a big bow on her head, she wore, for the first time, a white veil just like her older sisters.

It was the first time that Isabel had stepped outside her house since she had come back from the afternoon of Carnival fun the day before.

"Wow! Wow!" Isabel kept saying as she walked down the avenue, flanked by her father and two sisters. She couldn't believe the transformation that had taken place overnight. Indeed, her neighborhood seemed like a different place.

"This is a town with a hangover!" she exclaimed.

Her sisters giggled, and her father asked, "What are you talking about, Isabel?"

Isabel opened her arms and did a pirouette, pointing out, "Look! All the pretty banners ripped, the streets are full of garbage, and look at the trees!" The trunks of several of the rubber trees that divided the avenue into two lanes were vandalized with rotten eggs, ashes, and other undesirable wastes. The branches were full of confetti and broken balloons. As they went down the avenue, they saw a sandal jammed between two branches and several broken whiskey bottles.

"The town will clean this all up tomorrow." That was all that their father said, but Isabel was also observing the people who were walking to church. Like her family, everyone was wearing dark clothes. Whereas in other days there would be a lot of noise with people chattering and warmly greeting each other, today the "Good Mornings" were muttered and eyes were lowered.

"I wonder what *Nhõ* Padre is going to say about all this?" Fern said with a chuckle.

"A big tongue lashing from the pulpit for sure!" said Eliza.

"Shh! Be quiet, girls," their father said, obviously irritated by the girls' chatter.

In church, people sat by age group and sex. The very front of the church had wooden benches to each side, reserved for children. This is where Isabel usually sat. Today she sat with her sisters in the middle part of the church, which was reserved for young women. This is where the confessionals were, one on

either side. On Saturdays, you would sit and kneel
here, waiting your turn to go in. Isabel's father stayed
in the back part, reserved for men on the left and for
women on the right side. In this section, there were
no benches or kneelers. People stood up or knelt on
the floor. Many people, including her father, usually
opened up a freshly ironed handkerchief and laid it on
the dusty wooden floor so as not to get their knees or
pants dirty. Some people had their own chairs brought
from home. The only person who had a kneeler was
the wife of the island administrator. Her kneeler had
an attached arm rest, a *prie-dieu*. It was made of dark
wood and upholstered with maroon velvet, and it had
a plaque with her name written in brass.

"How pretentious!" Isabel usually thought,
but all the while she wished that her mother had a
prie-dieu just like that, and maybe if she had had one
she would have gone to church more often.

However, today she was not thinking about
any of these things. She was sitting in the middle
part of the church with her older sisters, and she was
wearing a brand new white veil. As she had seen her
Sunday school teacher do often times, Isabel, using
her two hands, brought the two ends of the veil up,
covering her mouth, and she let the veil rest there.

She closed her eyes and pretended that she was deep in prayer. She then opened her eyes and saw one of her girl friends, who was sitting in front with the children. Her friend gestured to her as if to say, "Who do you think you are sitting with the older girls?" Isabel shrugged her shoulder and went back to pretending to be in deep prayer.

"*In nomine Patris, et Filii, et Spiritus Sancti,*" the priest began. Isabel loved Latin and knew by heart the Kyrie, Gloria, Credo, Sanctus and Agnus Dei, and many such prayers. In their little island, they had three languages. Latin was for church, Portuguese was to read and write, and Crioulo was what everybody spoke. Isabel liked Latin the best, and Portuguese least. She put Portuguese in the same category as the administrator's velvet covered *prie-dieu*.

It was very hot inside. The church was crowded, and there was little ventilation. It was a common thing for several people to faint and have to be carried out of the church. Today Isabel herself thought that she was going to faint. She had not eaten since suppertime the night before. She had practically forgotten about her treasure hidden inside the hollow root of the peach tree, until the priest elevated the host and said, "*Ecce Agnus Dei*" (This is the Lamb of God). As soon as he said that, her coveted sweet in the hollow root of the peach tree flashed into her consciousness. Her stomach growled loud enough for Fern to give her a shove. Isabel couldn't help it. She couldn't concentrate anymore on what was going on up on the altar. She could only think of committing a sin by violating the fast. Isabel prayed. She prayed intensely. She asked the little girl to help her keep the fast and help her honor Jesus at that moment. Suddenly, she felt nauseated and sweaty, and her knees gave away under her. Isabel blacked out.

Isabel stirred and felt the presence of people shuffling about. She heard sounds in whispers that she could not comprehend. She opened her eyes slightly, and all that she could see were shadows. She rubbed her eyes and began to focus and realized that she was back in her own room and in her own bed. Nevertheless, she was puzzled and kept turning her head from one side to the other. With her eyes wide open, she examined every detail of the room, including her family, as if she were seeing them for the first time. She sat up quickly and looked around, asking, "Where is the little girl?"

"What little girl?" her mother replied.

"The little girl who took me to . . ." Isabel began, but stopped short.

"What little girl? And where did she take you?"[10] her mother asked. Mrs. Rodrigues was instantly reminded of what her oldest, married daughter, Leyla, who now lived in Portuguese Guinea, had told her. Leyla claimed that she had once seen an angelic little girl follow Isabel in the middle of the night when Isabel had gotten up to go to the bathroom. That was six years ago, but Mrs. Rodrigues always got a chill up her spine whenever she remembered Leyla's vivid account.

"What little girl? Answer me!" she insisted.

But Isabel tightened her lips and lightly shook her head saying, "I don't know." She lay back on her pillow, closed her eyes, and turned her head away from her mother's gaze. Mrs. Rodrigues sat on the bed motionless, absent-mindedly caressing Isabel's head.

Eliza came in with a bowl of *caldo d' ovo* (egg drop soup), "Eat this, Isabel. It will make you feel better. I think that you are not yet ready for fasting," she said brightly. Fern and Eliza told her how much excitement her fainting had caused in church, how her father had carried her home, and how they were about to call the doctor when she began to gasp and choke.

"Gasp and choke?" Isabel questioned.

"Just for little while, and then you were just asleep," Fern informed her.

"And how long have I been asleep?" she asked.

"It has been maybe twenty minutes. Mass is just now over," Fern said.

Isabel felt very strange. The little girl and the place where she had taken her were still very vivid in her mind. It seemed to Isabel that she had been gone for days! The aroma of the *caldo d'ovo* made her nauseated, and when she looked in the bowl, instead of seeing ribbons of yellow and white swimming in a shimmering sea of oil beads and spices, she could only see dirty water. Isabel gestured for the bowl to be taken away. Mrs. Rodrigues insisted that she try just a few spoonfuls, but Isabel's face became pale and sweaty.

"Aren't you hungry?" she asked.

"No," Isabel answered feebly.

"Can I have it, Mother?" Fern said, already licking her lips.

"Can I also have some?" Eliza asked. Mrs.

Rodrigues looked at her girls and nodded her head in resignation. Isabel looked away as her two sisters hungrily drained the bowl.

Isabel closed her eyes and turned towards the wall. She feigned going to sleep. Her mother bent down, kissed her, and gestured the girls to leave.

"I will be back in a little while to check up on you. Call if you need anything," her mother said. Nevertheless, as she started to go out of the room, she turned around and said, "About that little girl, you can talk about her, but only to me. Don't mention it to anyone else." She went out gently closing the door but leaving it ajar so that she could keep an eye on Isabel from her chair in the hallway, where she was set up to do some mending.

Chapter Seven

The Little Girl

Isabel remembered being all of sudden in darkness, but a little hand held hers tightly. They went slipping and sliding in a dark tunnel that got brighter and brighter. The wind in the tunnel was so violent that Isabel felt as though her skin were being ripped off her body. The little girl's body sheltered hers a little, and suddenly they were violently thrown out of the tunnel and fell breathlessly into what seemed to Isabel to be a fluffy bed that extended forever in all directions. They bounced up and down for a little while, and the little girl giggled in delight and exclaimed, "Well, how did you like that?"

Although Isabel's body had come to a full stop, her heart continued to bounce rapidly, and she couldn't catch her breath. She did not seem to be getting any air. She was in pain. Isabel rubbed and rubbed her chest and held her throat but to no avail. The little girl came close and touched her lightly, and instantly she was calm and peaceful.

"What did you do?" Isabel asked.

"Nothing," the little girl answered.

"You did something. What did you do?" Isabel demanded.

"I just reset you to Heaven time," she said, looking gently at Isabel.

"Heaven time? Am I dead?" Isabel asked alarmed.

"No, but you asked for my help back in church, remember?" she said simply.

"Oh! Oh!" Isabel responded now, recalling her craving for her hidden sweet while she was supposed to be preparing her heart to receive Jesus in Holy Communion. As soon as she remembered the sweet, it appeared in plain view for the two of them to see, inside its golden wrapper, inside the newspaper, and inside the hollow in the root of the peach tree.

"So, *that* is what you were contemplating trading for the Majesty of Our Lord? Hmm?" the little girl asked.

Isabel was speechless. Not only could she see

through the hollow in the peach tree, she could also see anything on earth that flashed into her mind. As soon as Isabel thought about anything, it presented itself in plain view. She thought about her mother and she saw her mother, she saw her house, and she saw the church. She could even see all the people inside the church. The little girl quickly touched her again and said, "Oops! I forgot," and she giggled again. Immediately Isabel's vision was limited, and she could see only the object of her near downfall. She tried to pick it up, but it oozed something awful, and it sent shocks of disgust through Isabel's system.

"How did you do that?" Isabel asked pulling her hands quickly back to her side.

"Nothing! I didn't do anything," the little girl answered, moving slightly away.

"Then why does it feel and smell so bad, and why does it make me feel so sick just by touching it?" Isabel asked.

"Earthly things are like that. They are worthless and foul when you compare them to what God has in store for you. And the sooner you realize what they are and what their purpose is, the better," the little girl said, now slowly elevating a good ways up from Isabel. Isabel had to look up to see her face.

"And what is this, if not a chocolate bar? And what is its purpose if not to be eaten and enjoyed?" Isabel asked.

"Good question, and this is why I answered immediately your plea for help, and this is why I brought you here," she said authoritatively. Isabel tried to go where the little girl was standing, but she couldn't. The little girl, noticing her attempt, told her, "This is as far as you are allowed to go for now. Lie down, make yourself comfortable, and listen carefully, as you have never listened before. What you decide to do with what I am going to tell you will determine your fate," the little girl said emphatically.

Isabel answered almost sarcastically, "This sounds very serious! I guess this is my day of reckoning. Two grand talks in one day. First, my mother with her story about some woman named Mina, and now you."

Isabel lay down flat on her belly with her arms anchoring her chin. She looked up at the little girl whose countenance had changed. Although she was still that little girl, her whole body was aglow, and it seemed that a light inside her was making her translucent. Isabel was mesmerized. She became focused and attentive to what she was hearing and seeing.

The little girl then said, "You are blessed, Isabel. God has been trying to get your full attention for a long time. You are sitting on a fence right now. You don't know what to do, what to think, or what to believe. However, God sees you and rewards you for your efforts. Remember your attempt to visit Jesus two years ago in church?" the little girl asked. Isabel lowered her face, and she felt the heat of embarrassment consuming her whole body. "It was the thought, the intent that mattered. The thought and the intent matters more than if you had managed to stay prostrated for months and months in that dark church," the little girl continued. Isabel could not move. She was paralyzed by the painful thought that her most intimate secrets and desires of her heart were being exposed just as her mother's wash was exposed to the sunlight when she laid it to dry in the fields. She felt that her soul was being bleached out by the gaze of those above.

"God also was very pleased with you when you tried to mortify yourself on the terrace of the cistern," the little girl said, and to that Isabel looked up in terror as she saw herself on her knees on the terrace gravel. She had been only nine years old. She had heard of how God loved those saints who suffered, who loved suffering, and who sought and created opportunities to suffer for God. She remembered longing to be loved by God like those saints, and she came up with this plan to kneel on the gravel floor and pray with the rosary for as long as she could stand it. This feeble attempt, as with the church visit, ended prematurely. She was almost caught in the act, and if she had been caught, she might have been made fun of and taunted. That's how it was in her country. If you had any perceived weakness, that would become the name by which you would be known. Isabel perhaps would have been known as St. Isabelita, and as soon as people would see her, they would call out, "Here comes St. Isabelita!" They would recount the episode over and over of her pathetic efforts to imitate a saint.

The little girl, seeing Isabel's thought immediately said, "But that did not happen. God spared you from the eyes of those who would have judged you and misunderstood you. God has always loved you, and you touch His heart by your attempts to seek Him."

"Nevertheless," Isabel whispered with her

eyes lowered, fixing her gaze on her little nails that were only tiny stubs left by her constant nibbling.

"Nevertheless?" the little girl asked inquisitively.

"Yes! Nevertheless! I never feel that I belong. I don't see any of my prayers being answered. I always feel awkward and am doing stupid things. My mind wonders a lot. I daydream about things. I can never manage to learn properly the tasks that my mother wants to teach me. And if my family and friends ever got a glimpse of what I think about, I would be the laughingstock of the family. I almost am. My parents are already worried about my future. I am too," Isabel answered defiantly.

"You are correct. You don't belong here, and for that matter, no one belongs here. Earth is a special place and souls who go to earth go for a specific purpose. Earth has a strange attraction for souls once they get there. They become as magnets, attracted to the earth's magnetic core. They forget where they came from and begin to think that earth is their permanent home," the little girl said.

Isabel nodded her head and said, "That is what my mother told me, but it is hard to understand, especially the part about suffering."

"But what is suffering if not the process of trading an earthly state for a heavenly one?" the little girl said, fixing her gaze upon Isabel, who had by now moved closer to Isabel.

"Hmm? What do you mean . . . trading?" Isabel furrowed her eyebrows.

"That is exactly what it is, but I should explain. Not all suffering leads to a heavenly state. Only the suffering that is willingly accepted and offered up to God for the purposes of enlightenment and salvation of oneself or of others. I should add that 'oneself' and 'others' are in fact one and the same," the little girl answered promptly

"Now I am really lost. What on earth are you talking about?" Isabel said, throwing up her arms into the air.

The little girl laughed, "What on earth am I talking about? I am talking about 'what in Heaven,' not 'what on earth.' "

"Don't make fun of me," a red-faced Isabel muttered under her breath.

"I am not making fun of you. What I am trying to say to you, dear Isabel, is that suffering, whether it comes in the form of illnesses, misfortunes, unfair accusations, betrayals, disasters, destitution, and

Irma Silva-Barbeau   85

in your case, going without something that you are really set on, is a means of attaining holiness for oneself and for others," the little girl explained.

"Attain holiness–what exactly is that?" Isabel asked.

"Suffering, willingly accepted and offered, as I have said before, helps the soul detach from the earthly body just enough to make room for the life of God, which is grace, to enter the soul. Suffering in this way, purifies the soul and helps it to return to God from where it came in the first place. Hence, you are here to do exactly that, help souls return to God. That is the only purpose of you being here. And how do you do that?" The little girl answered, again reading Isabel's thoughts, "You do that by living consciously, knowing that you are on a mission from God."

Isabel became very sad and said, "Suppose that things are the way you say, but how can a little person like me, living in this tiny island, surrounded by this vast ocean, do what you say? You know what our national pastime is? Our national pastime is going to the lookout points- the *miradoros*- to look at the sea for ships that pass by, to dream and long for the day that a ship will dock that will take us away, and then we go home and we go to sleep with our bags packed under our pillows." Isabel paused and waited for the little girl to react, but when no reaction was forthcoming, she continued. "I have heard my mother say that we are trapped here, and people here always are pining for something. Everybody here has someone who lives elsewhere across the sea. My mother says that it is our destiny to live in a perpetual state of longing–*sodade*. We long for the better world that we believe exists out there, we long for a better life, we long to have our bellies filled, we long to have our wounds healed, we long to have our voices heard, and we long to be a part of this earth and not feel like wretches looking for the world out there to bring us a handout."

There was a great silence. Then out of nowhere a guitar appeared in the little girl's hands, and she began to strum it and sing in a soft melancholic voice,

"Sodade, sodade, sodade de Nhã Terra. Sodade, sodade, sodade . . ." She sang for quite a while. Isabel wept.

Then the little girl stopped singing, but continued to strum the guitar softly. "Oh! Isabel. You are so right. Your people do live in a state of perpetual longing. When they are home, they long for the world outside, and when they are in the world outside, they long to be at home. Your poets and singers have almost exhausted this theme of *sodade*, and it will become famous someday," the little girl said, looking compassionately at Isabel. Isabel, still whimpering, did not respond.

Then as though a bolt of lighting had zapped her, the little girl jumped up and tossed the guitar into the air blurting out, "But, oh! Isabel, if only your people would sing *sodade, sodade, sodade* for GOD! Sing, Isabel!" She urged her, "Sing, *sodade, sodade, sodade,* and long for your God and for your heavenly home. Heaven is where your treasures are, where all the longings, and the emptiness will be satisfied. Then your tiny island would become truly *Greja na oceano*, the cathedral in the ocean, with its spires reaching up and sending sweet melodies directly to Heaven."

"I guess what I have felt sometimes was *sodade* for God, as you said," Isabel whispered in a whimper.

"Yes. Yes! But lately, as you are growing up, your *sodade* is becoming more for earthly greener pastures and the good earthly life," the little girl responded.

"You are talking about Carnival and the chocolate candy bar again? Aren't you?" said Isabel.

"All these things are good in and of themselves, but they are not to be taken too seriously or as real or worth longing for, for any amount of time. They are rest stops on the way," the little girl said.

"I don't understand what you are saying," Isabel responded.

The little girl moved closer to Isabel and said, "You and your family know all about rest stops."

"What on earth–oops! What are you talking about . . . rest stops?" Isabel responded.

The little girl began, "Every year when you and your family walk for a half day to Ferrero during cane cutting season, your parents have different spots where you all stop, have a drink of water, and sit in the shade for a while before continuing forward. Well, those little stops, those little drinks of water, and those times under the cool shade of a tree are your carnivals and your chocolate bars. They are there to give you rest, lighten your load, and refresh your spirit during your journey. It is not to be mistaken for the destination itself. Whereas, when your family goes to Ferrero, they never forget their final destination, souls on earth forget where they are going, and they get lost and many times manage to convince themselves that earth is it."

"Now that you have put it that way, it seems unthinkable that we would confuse our rest stops as Ferrero. We love Ferrero. It has beautiful water springs. When we are in Ferrero, we climb coconut trees. We get to eat mangoes, oranges, tangerines, and guavas ripe from the trees. There is always plenty of fish, lobster, and other shellfish that the fishermen trade with Father. We swim, we hike, we play all day, and there is no school and no chores!"

The little girl was now sitting next to Isabel quietly listening to her go on and on about how special a place Ferrero is. After a while, Isabel stopped her chatter, turned to the little girl, and said, "I am so sorry. I got carried away, but why are you looking at me that way?"

"I was just wondering, Isabel, how much you are willing to give so that the people whom you love, and even other people who you have touched and who will touch your life in the future, even in the most casual of ways, will not forget and confuse the *carnivals* and the *chocolate candy bars* of this world for Heaven itself. Compared to what God has prepared for you, your *Ferrero* looks like this." The little girl opened her arms and Isabel had a peek. Isabel was thrown back by the sight of her beloved Ferrero from a Heaven's view. Her body convulsed, and she embraced herself and rocked back and forth in pain.

The little girl put her arms around her and said, "Even the most luxurious and precious Ferreros of the whole world do not compare. Enjoy them as "rest spots" in the moment, but do not attach yourself to them or put any value on them. When you attach yourself too closely to anything on earth, you are enslaved and cannot get free. You must be free to commune with God, as that is where Heaven is."

Isabel frowned. "What is this all about? Are you still talking about the chocolate candy bar?" she asked quite bewildered.

"Yes!" The little girl nodded her head, and looking straight into Isabel's eyes, she continued, "Many souls on earth are too attached, too enslaved for them even to dream of the possibility of detaching themselves from earthly things. This is a serious, almost fatal disease—perpetual longing for possessions and control of earthly things that can never satisfy a soul. As far as the universe is concerned, this is the greatest tragedy of humankind because such attachments are the root cause of the worst and the most hideous cruelties and injustices of men towards men and towards the earth itself. But there are a group of souls whom God has chosen to help with this situation, and you are among this group."

"Me?" Isabel tried to laugh, but could only manage to make a shrieking noise. She jumped forcefully up on her feet, wanting to run, but managed only to bounce up and down as though she were standing on a mattress of air.

"Yes. You!" the little girl said categorically.

"But, but I am having trouble handling the littlest of temptations, and besides, my little attempts at self-mortification have failed outright, and my prayers are useless."

"Well, I am here, am I not?" the little girl said.

"I guess," Isabel admitted, shrugging her shoulders.

"But speaking of unanswered, useless prayers . . ." the little girl opened her arms.

Isabel was struck with awe at what she saw and cried out, "Well, that is my father! That is my mother when she was younger! And that is me!"

"That is right, Isabel. Your father would not be alive today if you had not prayed for his safety.

He and his horse would have been swept out to sea in that hurricane, but God spared him and took him to higher ground because you asked Him."

"But, my mother? I don't understand," a bewildered and tearful Isabel cried out.

"Well, your mother lost her own mother when she was, well about your age. Her father was always away. She felt lonely, but see how God wrapped His arms around her and gave her comfort and courage when she needed it the most?" the little girl explained.

Isabel was trembling and could only say, "And look at me."

"Yes, and look at you," the little girl said.

"I remember that! I was coming down the avenue in Dee's bicycle, and the brakes gave out. I thought that I was going to hit the tree," Isabel held her breath and then emptied her lungs in relief. "I ended up falling on a rare patch of soft grass and just scraped my knees," she said in amazement.

"Do you remember what you said when you thought that you were about to hit the tree?" the little girl asked.

"God save me!" she said.

"Indeed!" the little girl responded.

The two girls did not speak for a while. They sat together side by side, with their hands folded on their laps and their legs dangling in the air, on the massive bed of clouds where they had first landed.

"Okay," Isabel said finally.

"Okay what?" the little girl said.

"What do you want me to do?" she said.

"The question is, what does God want you to do?" the little girl said.

"Okay, what does God want me to do?" Isabel asked finally.

"He wants you to help Him bring souls to Heaven," the little girl responded matter of factly.

Isabel gave a deep loud chuckle and said almost sarcastically, "This seems a task for great saints, not for a little girl with a chocolate problem. Still, I'm curious. How does He propose that I do this?"

"God proposes that you do this by keeping yourself detached from the world. God wants you to live in the world but always to remember that you are not from the world. Your song of longing, your song of *sodade*, Isabel, should only be for Him, for Jesus, and for Heaven and not for any earthly thing," the little girl said.

"Okay. How do I keep myself detached from the world? Does God want me to join a convent when I grow up?" Isabel asked.

"No, a life in the convent would be too easy for you, Isabel. God wants you to be fully engaged in the world, yet detached. In other words, you are to live a passionate and exciting outward life, but your interior life is to be serene and totally dedicated to Him," the little girl explained.

"I don't understand," Isabel answered, scratching her head.

"You don't have to understand right now; you only have to agree to be God's helper," the little girl said.

"Will I suffer a lot?" Isabel asked.

"That is for God only to know, but as I have been trying to tell you, it is not how much you suffer, it is your intent and offering that matters," the little girl said.

"I have always felt something, and I often pretended and wished that I was one of God's great saints like Joan of Arc and the martyrs, but I also know that I am a coward when it comes to physical pain. But I guess that I can give up the carnivals and perhaps even some of the chocolates of this world, for love," Isabel responded, surprised by the words coming from her mouth.

"I will always be near you, and I have always been near you. I will always be there to help you, and God will always answer your prayers. That is a promise that our Lord made to all humanity when He was on earth, and He does not ever fail His promises," the little girl said.

"What shall I do with the chocolate? If I leave it where it is, it will rot. It seems a pity to let it go to waste. Someone should have it," Isabel said.

"Are you making an offering?" the little girl asked, looking intensely at Isabel.

"With all my heart," Isabel said.

The little girl brought the chocolate bar up and held it in the palms of both her hands. Rising, she lifted it up and said, "A sweet offering! A sweet oblation! You cannot imagine the graces that can be released to souls on earth by the simple giving up, in the spirit of love and mortification, of a chocolate candy bar."

"You are right; I cannot imagine. I am too small. My brain is too small to understand what you are saying. Please, show me. Show me what happens," Isabel asked.

The little girl opened her arms again, and Isabel fell prostate, blacked out, and woke up in her own the bed, where she was now thinking about all these things and wondering if it all had been a crazy dream.

Chapter Eight

Lent

The next day there was no more talk about fasting or Isabel fainting the day before. It was as if nothing had happened and everybody started his day as usual. Fern and Eliza were up at seven in the morning, had their breakfast, did their chores, and were sitting with their embroidery by the front portico facing the park by nine o'clock. Ida and Mandy had been up early and attended the morning session at the school. Mrs. Rodrigues was in the kitchen grinding corn for the day's meal. Gustavo had been out early, taking the animals to pasture. Maria was out fetching firewood. Mr. Rodrigues had left for *Ferrero* with the first streak of light in the east. Isabel had been awakened earlier by his horse, *Kalifa*, galloping out of the side entrance. She had followed the clip-clop of the horse's hooves as they rhythmically hit the cobblestone, until the sound was just an echo that faded away.

Isabel had gotten up that morning with everybody else. She did her chores and got ready for school. She attended the afternoon session of the only public school in town known as the *Scolona,* the Big School, which was a five-minute walk from her house. As usual, she would sit at the table with the family for lunch but then would excuse herself to get ready for school, which began at one o'clock in the afternoon.

Isabel had her routine. When she was all ready for school, she would hang her cloth book bag over her left shoulder, securing the black slate with her arithmetic homework with her left arm, and she would stand by the door of the little eating room. She would then extend her right arm, and with palm exposed, she would timidly say, *"Papa nhõ dan benson."* (Father, give me your blessing.) Her father, sitting at the head of the table, would raise his eyes towards her, and with his right hand still holding the knife that he was eating with, would nod his head and say, *"Deus dabo benson."* (God bless you.) Isabel would quickly close her hands, as if she had just caught the blessing, and would put it in her bag.

Today there would be no blessing. Her father was by then already in *Ferrero* having his own lunch with the farm crew. When he was away, Isabel always felt strange and empty, and she would then bless herself instead and head off to school.

In the stark light of day, the purple cloths hanging all around the walls of their house spoke to everyone of the somber season that they were in, but besides that, everything seemed the same. Yet for Isabel, the world had changed. She felt different. In the days that followed, she often thought about the little girl and wondered whether it was real or just a dream. She did not dare speak about this to anyone, not even to her mother, who appeared to be particularly interested in the "little girl." She avoided going near the peach tree. She was afraid of what she might find there in the hollow of the tree, or what she might not find. In fact, she avoided the backyard as much as she could and restricted her play to the park, the front of the house, or the schoolyard. She couldn't get the little girl out of her mind though. Often she would lie in her bed before going to sleep, and she would whisper and ask, "Little girl, are you real? Can you hear me now?" Nothing happened, and she would start the next day following her usual routine, almost.

On Fridays of Lent, she made an extra effort to make some offering. She did not fast outright, because she did not want her family to know that anything was different, but she gave up things. One of the things that she found easy to do without raising suspicion was to leave all or part of her school snack on a bench, on top of a wall in the avenue, or on a path where she was sure someone in need would find it. Food was scarce enough that whoever found it would be grateful. She would wrap the snack carefully in a piece of paper or corn husks and tie it with a string, and she would say happily, "A present for you!" as she deposited her little bundle and imagined the reaction of the person when they found the tasty snack.

Another thing that she did was to give other kids in her class a chance to shine. This she found most difficult because she took pride in always being the top student in her class, and she took great pleasure in raising her little right index finger as soon as the teacher asked a question. These days she was measured in doing so. If she got a sense that someone else knew the answer, she was slower to raise her finger.

Throughout Lent, Isabel faithfully attended

Sunday school every Sunday afternoon. She considered going to *Doutrina*, as they called it, as much of a social activity as a religious instruction activity. She particularly enjoyed recess time when they played "*da cu taco*" (a type of softball played with a ball made up of rolled up old socks), tag, hide-and-go-seek, "*pedrihna na mon*," (pebble in your hand) and other such games.

Once, a Sunday school teacher came up with a game of "poses." In this game, the children would strike a pose, and a group of judges, made up of other Sunday school teachers, would judge each child's pose. Whoever came up with the most innovative and most beautiful pose would win a prize. One time Isabel managed for a split second to stand up teetering on top of a ball, opening her skirt wide, like a fan. She smiled and bowed to the judges, and for that, she won first prize! Her prize was a box wrapped in beautiful shiny paper with a big bow. All the children gathered around Isabel in great expectation while she opened the box. She first opened the big box, and inside that box was another box, and inside of it was yet another box. It had almost ten little boxes, one inside the other, and in the middle of the tiniest box was a piece of hard candy. Isabel saved the candy, which later she split into tiny pieces by pounding it with a stone, so she could share the rare sweetness with her girlfriends.

But recess aside, *Doutrina* was usually very serious. Some Sunday school teachers used this time to evoke the fear of God and to impress upon the young minds the consequences of disobedience to God. For instance, failing to go to Mass on a Sunday was a mortal sin–a sin so grievous that if it went unconfessed before you died, you would go straight to hell. Once, a Sunday school teacher told them a story of a beautiful, sweet, loving, young woman who was very kind and pious and did everything that her parents told her to do. But one Sunday, she deliberately did not go to Mass, and she died before she had a chance to go to confession.[11] After her death, her friends knowing that she had missed Mass, prayed and prayed for her salvation, but she appeared to them engulfed by flames and said, "Do not pray for me anymore; I am already condemned." Isabel often thought about that story and would tremble in fear.

Another story that usually evoked dreadful shivers down Isabel's spine was the story of the burial of Martin Luther. Martin Luther was considered, at one time by the Catholic Church, to be the greatest heretic who had ever lived. According to the Sunday school teacher, Martin Luther went against the Pope and started his own false church, leading people astray.[12] Isabel's Sunday school teacher once told them that when Martin Luther's body was being taken to the cemetery, a huge band of black crows flew over the casket. When the casket was laid on the ground for the burial, the crows landed on the casket claiming every inch of it. The children would huddle together in terror as they heard such stories. Isabel had told her mother the story about Martin Luther, and her mother had assured her that it was all nonsense.

During Lent, there was very little play, and the emphasis was on the Passion of Jesus Christ. The children were being prepared for Holy Week. "Imagine, imagine!" the Sunday school teacher would tell them, raising his voice slightly as he paced back and forth in front of them with his hands folded tightly against his chest, staring into the distance as if he were describing to the children what he was seeing. "Imagine what it must have felt like on that first Holy Saturday. Jesus' friends were in shock. His mother was pierced with sorrow. Did some of them think that their friend Jesus was just an unusually kind man, a gentle man, and a holy man, but at the end, just a man, like everybody else?"

The children would answer in chorus, "No! No!"

"They must have been scared. They must have been confused. Their spirits must have labored with guilt. Would you little ones run away from Jesus when He needed you? Would you? Would you?" he would ask them, bringing his face close to those unfortunate enough to be sitting in the front row.

"No! No!" they would answer.

"What did Peter do?" he would ask them.

"He denied knowing Jesus," the children would answer.

How many times did Peter deny knowing Jesus?" he would ask. "Three times," they would answer.

"Yes, three times!" he would repeat, nodding his head repeatedly. "When did he deny him?"

The children would answer, "When the rooster crowed."

"And how many times did the rooster crow?" he would ask.

"Three times," the children would answer in unison.

Thus the children were drilled over and over on the events that took place during Holy Week. They knew by rote the details of Jesus' betrayal, condemnation, and crucifixion. The bad guys and the good guys were clear, and all the children would vow that if they had been there they would all certainly have been the Veronicas and the Simons of the Cyrene, not Peter or Judas.

Isabel was also secretly keeping a list of her transgressions on a crumpled up piece of paper that she kept hidden under one of the floor boards in the room where her father had once had a family store, but which now was being used as a storage room. She began the list after a Sunday school session where they discussed the coming of the Holy Week and the custom of making a *Juda*. The *Juda* was an effigy of a person, and it represented all traitors in the person of Judas Iscariot, who betrayed Christ.

She had asked her mother about Judas Iscariot afterwards, and her mother explained. "I don't know, Isabel, how this tradition of making effigies of Judas Iscariot began, but I believe that Judas Iscariot represents all of us, that is, every human being from the first one, Adam, to the last one that will ever live on this planet. We all had a hand in the Passion and

Crucifixion of Jesus." In her heart, Isabel understood clearly what her mother was saying, and she decided to keep a running tab of her own sins and failings in thoughts, words, and deeds.

As the Lenten season was coming to a close, the children began to plan and gather materials to make their *Juda*. There was always lot of discussion going on about who was going to make what. Usually they would have a family of *Judas,* complete with a mother, father, and children displayed on the roof of the kitchen facing the avenue. Fern was going to make a big Papa *Juda* and was after her father to give her some of his old clothes. Isabel was quiet about her *Juda*. She chose one of her own old dresses that she found in the family trunk and asked her mother for permission to use it. She asked Gustavo for a supply of horse hair, a forked branch of a tree, as well as a straight stick for the body frame and arms, and a papaya for the head. She was very specific about the dimension of the branch and the size and shape of the papaya.

"Please, get me a papaya like that one!" she told him as she pointed it out on a tree that lined the back wall of the barn. "And I would like one that is not yet too ripe, with the flesh still firm."

Chapter Nine

The Voice on Wednesday

On Wednesday of Holy Week, Isabel turned twelve years old. There was no fanfare, no cake, or special dinners. That was not their custom. Nevertheless, Isabel felt very special that day. She was happy and peaceful in quite a different spirit than she had been the previous Sunday, Palm Sunday.

"How can there be all this rejoicing when we know what is going to happen to Jesus in a few days? I don't understand," she had asked her mother.

"It is God's plan, Isabel. This is how it was prophesized that Jesus would enter Jerusalem, where he would be killed. It is hard for our human minds to understand, I know," her mother said.

"Why do we sing, 'Hosanna, Son of David?'

Isn't Jesus the son of God and also the son of Mary?"
she asked.

"Yes, Jesus is the Son of God and the son of
Mary," she explained and continued. "But it is very
important to know and understand that Jesus is also
a Davidic king. He came from the line of David,
the greatest of the Jewish kings. This is how it was
prophesized that the Messiah, Jesus the Christ, would
come, in the flesh, from the line of David. So when
we sing 'Hosanna, Son of David,' we are in effect
saying that this Jesus is the One whom God has sent
and the One that God had promised and the One fore-
told by the great prophets. Do you understand, Isabel?" her mother asked tentatively.

"Yes, I think so!" she said, dangling a branch
of the palm. Happily she hopped and skipped away
singing, "Hosanna, Son of David! Hosanna, Son of
David! Hosanna, Son of David!"

Mrs. Rodrigues shook her head and smiled;
with Isabel, she never knew what to expect. After a
question like that, sometimes there would be a string
of other questions and arguments, and sometimes
she would promptly accept her answer and go on her
way. This was one of those times, and her mother
was grateful.

On the evening of her birthday, something extraordinary happened. It took place when BaBa came that night to get his supper. BaBa suffered from a mysterious rare illness. He was homeless, spoke with a drawl that was hard to understand, and drooled profusely when he opened his mouth to say anything. He was dirty, his clothes were torn, and held together by strings. His legs were swollen and his feet were deformed by worms that he harbored under his toe-nails, which infested his flesh. He walked with great difficulty, often holding his pants with one hand and balancing his body with his other hand. His speech was so muddled that you could only pick up a few words here and there. This frustrated BaBa, and he would scream, opening his mouth wide, exposing his rotten teeth that had never known the presence of a brush or a cup of cool, rinsing water.

He usually arrived at the Rodrigues' house precisely as they were ending their supper. He would come in by the side service entrance and stand by the window. Often he would come in so quietly that no one would be aware of him until he brought his face really close to the window, opening his eyes and mouth wide, making that unearthly sound that only BaBa could make. The children would scream in fright.

A few times Mr. Rodrigues had warned him that if he continued to frighten the children like that, he would not be welcomed anymore, but BaBa couldn't help it, and the Rodrigues did not have the heart to withhold his supper. This night, when all her siblings yelled out in fright at the sight of BaBa, Isabel stayed quietly in her seat. She didn't even blink and calmly asked Maria if she could hand over BaBa's supper through the window. Maria hesitated and looked to Mrs. Rodrigues. Mrs. Rodrigues nodded her head, and Isabel quickly got up from her seat, took the plate of food from Maria, went over to the window, and handed the plate and spoon to him. She even consciously touched his hand and said, "Eat up and enjoy, BaBa. Today's stew is especially good." BaBa screamed in gratefulness, and a gust of drool blew over the food; Isabel felt a drop in her hand. She said nothing and wiped it away on the lap of her skirt. BaBa sat as usual on the stone wall that divided the side service entrance from the fields and quietly ate. He left with the wind. No one noticed.

Isabel's sisters, Maria, and Mrs. Rodrigues

were puzzled at Isabel's action. "Weren't you scared to go up so close to him?" Ida asked.

"He smells bad," Mandy chimed in.

Isabel did not know what to say about why she did what she did, but as she was leaving the dining room, she looked back at her family and said, "No. I was not frightened; after all, he is just like us." Mrs. Rodrigues frowned and the others looked at her with open mouths.

However, BaBa was not the only such person whom Isabel had been befriending secretly during Lent. There was a man who had been born with deformed arms and hands. He had just stubs for arms with deformed little fingers. He lived beyond the mountains but came to town everyday begging. He wore old, dirty, patched up clothes. He carried a sack across his shoulders with an open flap for people to slip in donations of food and money. He played a harmonica as he walked all over town. In typical fashion of the townspeople, no one knew his name, only what distinguished him -his deformed arms and hands. So he was called Mr. Little Hands. One day when Isabel saw Mr. Little Hands coming up the avenue from the direction of the church, she skipped casually to the sidewalk, pretending that she was practicing hopscotch. As Mr. Little Hands passed by, she said, without taking her eyes from the invisible hopscotch squares, "How sweetly you play your harmonica!" Mr. Little Hands was startled. He stopped his playing for a second and looked at Isabel. Isabel looked up, and their eyes met for a moment. Mr. Little Hands started again on his march, now playing his harmonica with renewed animation.

There was also another beggar who was unusually tall, and Isabel did not know where he came from, but he was often seen in the park area. He used to go house-to-house, begging. His name was Mr. Tallman. One day as Mr. Tallman was in the park, Isabel came close to him and said, "When I grow up, I want to be as tall as you. I heard that tall people like you come from royalty. You must be royal!" Mr. Tallman raised his brow and gave out a loud chuckle. He continued on his begging route, but with a different spring in his step.

Then there was Miss Mary. Miss Mary was mentally ill and spent a lot of her time in church. You would hear her coming up the avenue because she had the habit of holding her rosary extended out in one hand and saying her rosary aloud as she went about town. Isabel, hearing Miss Mary coming up the avenue, sat on one of the steps that went up to the park, directly on Miss Mary's path. As Miss Mary passed her by, Isabel said, "You pray the rosary so well. Your prayers must be powerful. Please pray for me?" Miss Mary continued on her litany of Hail Marys uninterrupted, yet for a minute turned around towards Isabel, walking backwards and raised her rosary arm towards her.

That night, the night of her birthday, the image of BaBa, and her own words–*He is just like us*–kept playing over and over in Isabel's mind. *BaBa, Mr. Little Hands, Mr. Tallman, and Miss Mary are the untouchables in the community. People speak about them with pity–they are the unfortunate, the destitute, but they are never considered to be like us. If not like us, who are they like?* Isabel thought as she lay back in her bed. She looked at the spot where BaBa's drool had touched her hands earlier that evening. She remembered how his skin felt under her finger tips–*a little rough but like everybody else's.* She thought of the little girl and whispered, "Help me understand."

It was then that she heard a voice, just as she was about to fall asleep, that said, "They are just like you because they are part of me. Thank you for supper, and for your comforting words." It was a voice unlike any other voice that she had ever heard before. The voice was loud, but gentle to the ear. It was inside of her head, but it was also outside. She quickly sat up in bed and looked around to see if anyone else had heard it, but Ida and Mandy were deep asleep.

"Who are you?" she asked in a whisper. There was only silence.

Isabel looked up at the crucifix that hung over her bed, covered up by the purple cloth. She whispered in awe, "Thank you, my sweet Jesus," and with that thought, she surrendered her body and fell quickly asleep.

Chapter Ten

Judas on Holy Thursday

On Thursday morning of Holy Week, the day after her birthday, Isabel was overtaken by a deep somberness. The Sunday school teacher's daring to "imagine" how it must have felt to be present in Jerusalem consumed her, and she began to ponder the events. She was sitting on a stool in the kitchen courtyard silently assembling her *Juda*.[13] The household was in a very gregarious mood. The courtyard was a hub of activity with all the children working on their *Judas*. There were mounds of straw to fill the bodies, dried banana trunk strips to tie the frames, green papayas of all shapes, ripe coffee beans, corn cobs, old shoes, hats, dresses, pants, shirts, coats, and anything else that the children were able to dig out from the old family trunk. Gustavo was the principal assistant, helping the girls cut the

A-frames from the tree branches and sticks for arms into the right size, carving the faces out of the papayas, and making pipes out of dried corncobs.

Isabel had asked for very little help. She really did not have a plan in her head of what she was doing. She only knew that she wanted to do it by herself. First, she got the frame all set and tied a straight stick at the joint across the A-frame for arms. She then carefully wrapped the frame surface with strips of dried banana tree trunk, and she put it aside. Next, she began working on the head. With a sharp knife, she peeled a portion of one side of the papaya for the face. Around the cheeks, she carved it into deeper layers to expose the rose flesh of the fruit in the first stages of ripening. She wanted the cheeks to be rosy. She carved two holes for the eye sockets, a nose, and ears. Although most *Judas* are depicted smiling with a gaping mouth full of teeth of stone or sticks, Isabel's *Juda* had a small mouth with marks only to show the lips tightly sealed. Then she got horse hairs and started to fix individual hairs by pressing them into the flesh of the papaya. She wanted her Juda to have long black hair and a face framed with thick black bangs. She put the head aside and dressed the frame, then began to fill it with straw under the dress. She had a hand full of fine straw, and as she was about to fill the left side of her *Juda's* chest, when the thought came to her. She quickly put the frame aside and rushed inside the house without being noticed. She went to the storage room and retrieved the crumpled paper with the list of her transgressions from under the floorboard. She swiftly inserted the ball of paper inside the fine straw and secured it in the left side of the *Juda's* chest. She continued to fill the dress with straw, and then she secured the head with eyes of dark, ripened coffee beans onto the frame. As soon as she did that, Mandy yelled out from across the courtyard, "Isabel's *Juda* looks like her!" Everyone looked in her direction.

"Are you making a *Juda* of yourself?" asked Fern. Isabel had not thought about it.

"I guess. It looks a little like me. She has my old dress on."

"It looks nice, Isabel. It is very clever of you," Eliza said, nodding her head in approval.

By late afternoon, all the *Judas* was ready for display. Mr. Rodrigues helped Gustavo raise each *Juda* individually up onto the kitchen terrace. The children gave Gustavo directions on how to group the *Judas* and display them. Isabel wanted her *Juda* to be standing next to the mother *Juda* and in front of Eliza's. The family of *Judas* was to be displayed for the public throughout Good Friday. The whole family went outside to see how their *Judas* looked and make final changes in the arrangement. Everyone was surprised and amused with his handiwork. Although no one verbalized it, each recognized himself in the group. The family was complete with the two boys, Andy and Joseph, who were away at school, big sister Leyla and her husband Oliver, and, of course, Gustavo and Maria.

Isabel went with her family to the Holy Thursday service in the evening and began to think about the events of that first Holy Thursday long ago. She tried to put herself in the actual scene, as her Sunday school teacher had suggested. Sometimes she felt herself as one of the apostles, sometimes she was Mary, and then sometimes she was Jesus. She felt most like herself when she tried to put herself in the place of the apostles, because, although they were all grown men like her father, they acted more like children. They seemed to understand very little of what was going on and had little clue as to what was ahead of them. When she tried to put herself in the place of Mary, she felt like her mother–someone with greater understanding. To put herself in the shoes of Jesus was most difficult. She prayed a lot.

That evening, sitting at the supper table with her family, Isabel asked herself, "How would I feel right now if I knew that this was my last meal, if this was the last time that I would sit around this table with this group of people whom I love? How would I say goodbye to them?"

Jesus said goodbye to his disciples at the Last Supper, but they did not understand. In fact, it was an awesome goodbye. He told them that by remembering Him in the bread and wine, they could drink Him and could eat Him, and in essence, carry Him within themselves all the time. He also showed them how they should take care of each other, but they did not understand right then and there. They were children, and like children, they had to grow up to remember the lessons of childhood and understand.   Isabel was constantly fighting off tears throughout that evening as she pondered these things. She went to bed that night, but not before she hugged and kissed her parents and touched lightly the arms of each one of her sisters. She felt like she also was saying goodbye to those whom she loved, but where was she going? She did not know, but she knew for sure that she was on a journey. By tomorrow she would not be there in the same way, if not in body, in spirit, perhaps.

The last thought that Isabel had before she fell asleep was a prayer, *"Let me help you, Jesus. Help me understand what happened this night so many years ago."*

In her dreams, Jesus took her to the garden of Gethsemane where He prayed alone before He was taken by the Roman guards. She was suffocating and felt her chest being crushed rib by rib by the weight of the world's sins. She cried out. She struggled, but the weight got heavier and heavier. She felt her body sinking deeper and deeper into the earth. She couldn't cry out, she couldn't move, and she couldn't breathe. She wished for death, but it would not come. Then she felt a hand lifting her up to the surface, and she finally woke up, sweating and gasping for air. She sat up in her bed and heard the cock crow. "Yes, I know him! Yes, I know him! Yes, I know Him!" she yelled out, but no one heard her. She fell back on her bed, and the exhaustion claimed her instantly.

Chapter Eleven
Spiders on Good Friday

On Good Friday, she woke up to the call of her mother.

"Wake up, Isabel! Wake up!" Mrs. Rodrigues was desperately trying to get her daughter up. Isabel just moaned and groaned and would not budge.

"Wake up. It is time to get up. Everyone else has been up for hours. Don't you want to participate in the killing of spiders?" her mother finally asked.

"Killing of spiders?" Isabel managed to open one quizzical eye, but felt her body too heavy to move.

"Your sisters are searching for them in the barn," her mother said.

"Oh! Oh!" Isabel at last came to and realized what day it was.

There was a custom on her island of killing

spiders on Good Friday. No one seemed to know where this custom came from or the reason for it. But the custom was so ingrained in the culture that often if someone did you wrong, or if you found yourself in need and asked someone for help and they refused you help, then you would warn them by saying, "Each spider has its Friday!"

Spiders are considered a bad omen, and somehow this was linked with the horror of Good Friday. On this day, you would seek to get rid of spiders, as a symbol, perhaps, of getting rid of everything evil or sinister. So it was the custom that on the morning of Good Friday, children armed with sticks go on a wild spider hunt. The horse barn was the prime site for the spiders. Usually the ceiling of the barn would be thick with webs housing huge black spiders with bright yellow stripes across their bellies. On Good Friday, though, one would be hard pressed to find them.

Fern came in disappointed and complaining, "It is as if someone tipped them off. All those spiders that were in the barn yesterday have disappeared." The hunt had more to do with the chase than with the "killing." Nevertheless, a few unsuspecting spiders would be sacrificed.

Isabel was not in the mood for the spider chase this morning. Her body ached, and she could hardly move. Her mother got a hold of her arm to spring her up from bed, but Isabel burst into a wild scream as if she were in excruciating pain.

"What is wrong?" her mother asked, startled by the scream. "Nothing. It is nothing, really," she responded promptly, moving her arm as though trying to get a cramp out. She did not want her mother to be alarmed. "I am getting up. I will be downstairs in a minute," she smiled, reassuring her mother.

"Okay then," her mother said, looking inquisitively at Isabel.

Isabel sat in bed and continued to smile until her mother was out of sight. She was in great pain. Her body ached and the joints of her wrists, her elbows, and her knees were particularly sore. Her head hurt, and she felt so weak that she could hardly manage to get her clothes on.

"Killing of spiders," she murmured to herself. "This must be the insane day that mother spoke about–the day when the unthinkable happened. The day when evil whispers in the wind told the body that it could be God and tried to oust the spirit. This is the day that the wind from the east managed to whisper to the house and made it think that it could be the master. Killing of innocent spiders must be a vestige of this cruel day. We children are made to taste the fury of a mob set to destroy, to victimize, to create pain in the innocent." Isabel moaned and slowly went downstairs for breakfast.

At breakfast she could not eat. "I am going to try to fast today," she told her mother. "I have not been able to fast all Lent long, so this is my last chance. Okay, Mother?"

"Okay, but if you feel that you are getting sick or going to faint, you tell me right away," her mother consented.

"I am not going to faint. I am certain that this time I am going to succeed." She smiled with confidence at her mother.

They could hear the other children in the courtyard boasting about how many spiders they had killed. Isabel did not want to be involved in any of that today.

She wanted to go out to have a look at their family of *Judas* on the kitchen terrace, but it had started to drizzle, unusual for this time of the year. The fog that usually covered the mountain peaks in the early hours of the morning had lingered, and the sky was overcast. The hot sun did not come out as usual to chase the fog away. It began to rain even a bit more.

In most days, from the window where she now stood, she could see the sparkling blue waters of the Atlantic Ocean and the neighboring island of Fogo with its imposing volcano, but not today. Now she could only see the park and nothing else. The mountains that surrounded the town and everything else were enveloped in the dense fog.

From the window, she could see a few people dressed in black going to church. Black and other subdued colors were the only acceptable colors to wear this day. The color red was never worn on this day. Red was for the unbelievers and appropriate only for a *Juda*.

With the spider killing fury over, everything was supposed to be done quietly. There would be no singing or any loud noise. Throughout the day, children would be shushed by the adults whenever they forgot and broke into a song or got into raucous play. The church bells also would be silent until Easter morning.

Isabel's thoughts touched Jesus.' He was already condemned. He was carrying the cross on the streets of Jerusalem. She envisioned Him and a crowd passing by her window. Would she really be courageous like Veronica and offer to wipe His face? Would her father step up from the crowd, like Simon of Cyrene, and help with His cross? She ached and doubled over in sorrow. She was interrupted by Gustavo shouting something to Mr. Rodrigues. He had climbed the terrace, pulling a big canvas that they used to protect the crops when they were being dried. Mr. Rodrigues handed him some sticks, and he began to make a tent protecting the *Judas* from the rain.

"They won't burn if they get wet," Mr. Rodrigues shouted to Gustavo. "Secure the canvas well with the rocks. Otherwise, the wind will blow it away." Gustavo secured the canvas at the edge with four big rocks as Mr. Rodrigues instructed.

Isabel watched the men until they were both inside the house. She sat there looking dispassionately at the fog and the rain. She had no energy. She was listless and her stomach growled. It was approaching lunchtime, and since practically everyone was fasting, the household would spend the lunch hour in their beds, resting. Isabel joined her sisters for a long afternoon nap.

She was awakened by the sound of voices.

At first, she did not realize what it was; then it was clear that it was voices of people chanting. She sat in bed alone, listening. Her sisters were already up. She jumped out of bed, but quickly retrieved a blanket to wrap around her shoulders. There was a cold, strong draft in the house. She now could hear clearly the chant,

Hail Mary, full of grace, the Lord is with thee. Blessed are thou amongst women, and blessed is the fruit of thy womb, Jesus. Holy Mary, Mother of God, pray for us sinners, now and at the hour of our death. Amen.

It was the Good Friday procession passing in the avenue. Her mother had opened all the windows in the house facing the avenue and had draped them with the family's best and most beautiful bedspreads and tablecloths. This was to honor the procession, to fill the house with the faithfuls' prayers, and to receive the Blessed Sacrament. The priest walking behind the cross was holding the monstrance with the consecrated host. The altar boys dispensed incense, which saturated the air and the odor hung in the dense fog. Isabel joined her family as they all stood reverently at the window, joining with the crowd in their prayers.

They stayed there in the window until the last of the procession participants passed by and the flickering of the candles disappeared in the fog. The chanting, however distant, was heard phasing in and out, depending how far or near the procession passed. The family sat quietly. Isabel felt pain in her wrists and ankles. She had asked to understand what went on that day thousands of years before, and she felt privileged to feel something. She whispered to herself, *Miserere nobis* (Have mercy on us.)

That evening Mrs. Rodrigues served a simple fish soup for supper. While her family ate the soup hungrily, Isabel only wet her lips. She was not hungry. She was in no pain anymore. She felt numb. That night she slept peacefully.

Chapter Twelve

Bonfire on Holy Saturday

Isabel sat alone on the low concrete wall that fenced in the flower garden in front of her house. She was supposed to be in the park with her younger sisters, playing while waiting for supper, but she did not feel like playing. She wanted to savor the solitude. So, her sisters went ahead with the agreement that they would play in the park area nearest the house where she could hear them.

"Holy Saturday afternoon!" she murmured. The deed had been done; Jesus was dead and buried.

Isabel trembled at these thoughts. She brought her knees up against her chest and covered her legs with her dress skirt. She buttoned her sweater and curled into a ball. She let herself fall back and rested against the corner columns of the concrete fence. Her face was still flushed from the blaze of that morning's bonfire. The bath afterwards had cooled her body down, and the clean clothes shielded her hollow frame. Like the *Judas* that they had made, she felt like she had no form. All the stuffing had been burnt out of her. She felt empty, tired, but at peace. Since her birthday, only three days ago, she felt that she had been sucked down into the earth's core, then spewed out along with the ashes through the volcano's crater, and had fallen into the cool waters of the Atlantic. She felt like she was there now, listlessly bobbing up and down, waiting for the waves to take her eventually to shore. Perhaps she was waiting for something else. She did not know; she was waiting, just like her Sunday school teacher had told them that Jesus' mother and apostles had done—waiting and not understanding what had happened or why. Although they waited in fear, Isabel was not anxious or worried. She felt utterly exhausted.

The morning fog had lifted, but most of the day had been overcast. Now in mid-afternoon, the sun broke periodically through the clouds. The warmth on her cheeks took her back to the events of that morning.

Early on Holy Saturday morning, the household awakened with the excitement of the bonfire. Gustavo had cleared a big area in the cornfield behind the house and had collected straw, corn stumps, dried cow dung, and firewood. Now it was ready. He had a mound with cornhusks and cow dung, and tented over the mound, he set up the kindling and then the bigger pieces of firewood. He and every member of the family made a procession, each carrying his own *Juda*. Isabel carried hers behind Eliza. They all stood in a circle around the bonfire, and Mr. Rodrigues and Gustavo began to pile the *Judas* one on top of the other. There was also a pile of sticks, one for each person. Mr. Rodrigues gave Gustavo the signal. He lit the kindling and the whole mound slowly was set ablaze. They stood at a distance watching the *Judas* burn in total silence.

The whole island was participating in this ritual. In fact, if one were to stand on top of the highest mountain peak, one would see the island dotted all the way down to the sea with sparkles of fire. The death of Jesus was the event that each person was remembering by beating the blazing *Judas* with his or her stick, saying, "This is for killing Jesus. This is for killing Jesus." They struck the effigies until there were no more flames, just a pile of ashes and smoke from the green wet wood. Isabel was crying, but no one noticed. Everyone's faces were dirty from the ashes that flew in the air and red from the glow of the blaze. She stood there quietly watching. Then she took her own stick as the flames were dying down, and began to beat what remained of her own *Juda,* crying out between sobs, *"Mea culpa. Mea culpa." (My fault, my fault.)"Ignōsce! Obsĕcro, mihi ignōscas!"* (Forgive me! Please, forgive me!)

"What are you saying, Isabel?" Gustavo shouted. He was watching the children carefully, trying to keep them at a safe distance from the flames.

Isabel did not hear him and continued to strike the remains of her Judas repeating, *"Mea culpa. Mea culpa. Ignōsce! Obsĕcro, mihi ignōscas!"*

Gustavo came closer to Isabel and moved her back.

"Not so close," he said. By then most of the family members had left the bonfire area. At last, Isabel threw her stick into the dying bonfire and followed her family towards the house. They all had gathered on the terrace of the cistern where Mrs. Rodrigues was waiting with buckets of water, soap, and towels.

Isabel huddled up in her sweater. She could

hear her sisters playing in the park, but they would be returning soon. It was almost suppertime. She looked at the sun: it was now a sliver behind the horizon, leaving a glow that painted the western sky a deep orange behind the mountains. Isabel thought, *Easter has begun somewhere in the world.* Her eyes overflowed with tears and droplets coursed down her cheeks as she remembered all that had taken place since her birthday on Wednesday. She took a deep breath and decided to check on her sisters.

Just at that moment, she heard Ida calling from the steps going up to the park, "Isabel, Isabel, come and see something. Quick!" She gestured with her arms for Isabel to make haste. "Come! Quickly, quickly!" she shouted with impatience.

Isabel quickly dried off her face and ran up the steps towards Ida. "What? What is happening?" she asked Ida, a bit alarmed.

Ida was out of breath and excited, and she pointed, "Look! Look at Mandy!"

"What?" Isabel asked as they ran towards Mandy. Mandy was balancing herself on the second square of the hopscotch with her tongue sticking out, and then she hopped to the first square to finish her first complete round without an error. The town elec-

tricity, which kicked in at precisely six o'clock, illu-
minated Mandy's spot.

"Good, Mandy. Now show Isabel how good
you are," Ida encouraged her to continue.

"That is wonderful, Mandy," Isabel said as
she patted her little sister on the back. Mandy stood
straight in front of the first square. She held the
smooth stone with her right hand and kissed it for
good luck. She threw the stone right in the middle
of the first square and hopped over on her right, bare
foot to the second square. She continued hopping all
the way to the head and back to the second square.
She stopped there, balancing herself on one foot. She
bent over and picked up the stone, hopping safely
back to the cheers of her sisters.

"Let me continue to finish a round," a proud
Mandy said.

As she was focusing to throw the stone on the
second square, Maria yelled out from the window,
"Isabel, Ida, Mandy! Time for supper!"

"Oh!" a disappointed Mandy said.

"It is all right. You can show us tomorrow!"
Isabel said. The girls started out towards the house.

"I wonder what is for supper." Mandy asked.

"The same as everyday," Ida replied.

"*Jagasida* (steamed ground corn with lima beans and kale) and fish stew," Mandy answered, disgruntled.

"Maria told me that Mother has two chickens ready for tomorrow, and also rice!" Ida added.

"Rice? Where did Mother get the money for rice?" Mandy asked. "I don't know, but Maria said that Mother sent her to the store this morning to get some for tomorrow. Also, she said that we are even going to have dessert!" Ida said. They walked in silence, and as they were stepping inside the garden to the house Ida said, "I am so glad that Lent is over– all that going to church."

"And all that fish stew!" Mandy added.

"Aren't you glad Lent is over, Isabel?" Ida asked.

"I am just glad for Easter," Isabel replied.

Chapter Thirteen
Glory on Sunday

The bells of St. John the Baptist Church began to ring relentlessly with the first light. The sun kissed the earth and pulled open the curtain of gray, exposing a mantle of sparkling blue. The sea mimicked the sky, and from across the ocean, houses could be seen as little white dots on the volcanic island of Fogo.

Mrs. Rodrigues, Gustavo, and Maria were up with that first bell. Gustavo killed the chickens, and Maria dunked them in a cauldron of hot water and began to pluck and clean them. Mrs. Rodrigues prepared breakfast. Today there would be eggs, fried leftover *jagasida*, and coffee.

Isabel woke up and listened to the bells. The room was still dark, but rays of light penetrated the thick wooden shutters bolted against the windows for the night. She looked up from her bed and her heart fluttered as she saw the shiny cross on the wall over her bed. She stood on the bed, caressed the cross, and whispered, "Hello."

"Hello? What kind of prayer is that?" Ida said as she lay lazily in bed watching her sister.

"I am just saying hello to a friend that I have not seen for a long time." Isabel answered.

Ida rolled her eyes and shook her head. She had a hard time understanding her sister sometimes, but she just said, "Mother was here earlier. She pulled off the purple cloths and probably already has stashed them all away for next year."

"When are the bells going to stop? They woke me up!" Mandy complained, rubbing her eyes and pulling the bed sheets up to her chin.

"They will probably continue until time for Mass. Isn't it nice to have some music at last?" Isabel said.

Eliza came in and immediately began to open the shutters, flooding the room with the golden sun and the loud, hollow sound of the bells.

"Get up! It is Easter! We have to start getting ready for church. Ida, Mandy, go down stairs. Mother has something special ready for breakfast.

We have to wait until after church," she said as she looked at Isabel. That was a hard and fast rule that every Catholic child knew by heart: To receive Holy Communion, you had to be in a fasting state from midnight until the hour of Communion.

"Isabel, have you seen your dress and your sisters' dresses?" Eliza asked with a special gleam in her eyes. "Mother has just finished ironing them. You three will have the most beautiful Easter dresses on the whole island!" she said with pride. Mrs. Rodrigues, Eliza, and Fern had been working on the identical dresses for months. The dresses were white with bright yellow appliqué on the hem and chest. Embroidered on the appliqué were little chicks in a patch of grass and wild flowers. Eliza did the appliqué, Fern did the embroidery, and Mrs. Rodrigues sewed the dresses. The dresses were very short.

"The latest style," Eliza had insisted. The three girls would also be wearing white knee socks with freshly polished white shoes. Their long hair would be tied in a ponytail with a big white bow. Isabel's older sisters doted on her and their two youngest sisters. Isabel went along and let herself be decorated, but she paid little attention to all the fuss.

The park was a hub of activity by eleven

o'clock. The park divided the long avenue that ran from east to west, covering the entire length of the plateau where the town was situated. At its eastern end, there was a *miradoro,* called *Cruz Grande*, because it was in a shape of a ship with a big cross on its bow. It overlooked the sea and the island of Fogo. The avenue ended at the foot of the mountains at its western side. The park was the heart of the town, where everything of note took place. In the center of the park was a big gazebo, where on days like today, there would be music blasting in the afternoon for the pleasure of the park goers. Otherwise, it served as a pulpit for political speeches and dissemination of island news. From the gazebo, the park extended outward in a circle. At the edge of this circle were paths where young people walked around and around. The girls usually walked in one direction and the boys in another, and it provided a venue for discreet courting in the Portuguese colonial style. From this inner circle, the squared park rounded in four corners by what the locals called the "half oranges." The "half oranges" were semicircles with orange sections designed on the ground. Cement benches bordered these semicircles for people to sit. The sheltered area of the half oranges served as a safe area for young children to play. Behind the half oranges were beautiful, carefully-tended flower gardens, which gave the park its outer square design. Each of the four corners was separated from the others by wide entrances, which led into the street. The Rodrigues' house was precisely at the eastern entrance.

The Church of the Nazarene, the first Protestant church on the island, also overlooked the park at its northern entrance. On Sundays and especially today, the singing from the church saturated the air in town and echoed back from the mountains.

"There is one thing about the Protestants, they sing a lot and also loudly," Mrs. Rodrigues at one time had pointed out.

That was one thing that Isabel wished that they would do more in her church. "Why don't we sing like the Protestants?" she asked her Sunday school teacher one day.

"We are different from the Protestants. Our Mass recalls the sacrifice on the Cross. We are a Eucharistic people," he said and walked away, not wanting to discuss or entertain the possibility of any virtues that the Protestants might have.

We are a Eucharist people. We believe that Jesus Christ lives in flesh and blood in the conse-

crated host, and the Protestants don't. Isabel understood that. That single fact had been drilled in her head
since the first day that she attended Sunday school.
Shouldn't that be a reason to sing? She thought.

She loved to sing and knew many of the
songs that the Nazarene Protestants sang just from
hearing them Sunday after Sunday. She found them
uplifting and fun, and besides, her best friend Dee,
was a Protestant. Isabel even secretly visited Dee's
church one day. Isabel was so scared that she thought
she was going to die of a heart attack and go straight
to hell for stepping inside that church. It was strange,
but she found her friend's church cool and peaceful
inside. It had no pictures, no statues, and no candles
like her church. It looked to her more like a school
than a church, with plain benches all lined up.

Today the Protestants were singing with
unusual gusto. They were celebrating Easter just
like the Catholics, but according to her friend, they
did not believe in suffering and all that Lenten self-
mortification. That was one of the many points that
distinguished her faith from that of her friend's, and
she imagined that was one of the points of the many
arguments that her father would consistently have
with his Protestant friends in the park.

The streets were filled with people dressed in their Easter Sunday best. Everybody was going to church–the Protestants crossing the park in one direction with their Bibles piously under their arms, and the Catholics crossing the park in another direction, reverently clasping their rosaries.

The bells from Isabel's church and the choir from her friend's church filled the air with praise and thanksgiving, and along with the blue sky, sunshine, flowers, and birds singing, it gave the feeling, at least in Isabel's mind, that God was pleased with everyone.

She went to church with her sisters and father. Mrs. Rodrigues, as usual, stayed home. This bothered Isabel a little. Her mother was always saying that she was too busy or did not have the "proper" clothes. Once Isabel had overheard her mother talking with one of her cousins about some things about the priests and the church that she didn't think were right. Isabel didn't quite understand what they were talking about, but she always thought that they were the main reasons why her mother preferred to pray at home. Isabel reasoned that this maybe one of those things that her mother meant when she always said,

"When you grow up you will know, and you will decide for yourself."

Easter lunch was a feast indeed. Mrs. Rodrigues had prepared a delicious *"canja,"* a special chicken soup, with rice and linguiça. There were also chicken and potatoes sautéed in butter, rice with paprika, and fresh young lima beans, and salad with lettuce and cherry tomatoes fresh from the garden. For dessert, there was Mrs. Rodrigues's *goyabada*, a special sweet made of guava fruit.

After lunch, everybody lay down for a nap. Afterwards, the Rodrigues family would take a short walk to Lem, where her father's family lived, to visit his sister and some of their elderly relatives. This was a Sunday ritual, and the children dreaded this, as they had to kiss all those old people. Going to Lem on Sundays was a "duty" her mother would often say when the children protested. "Duty is not supposed to be fun," she would add.

On this day, Isabel understood that in this "duty" there was an opportunity to obtain grace. This thought occurred to her as she was bending down to hug and kiss her father's great-aunt, who was an invalid. The children always pulled back because her kisses left dabs of saliva all over their faces.

"Don't pull back!" a voice in her head told her. "Give yourself to her. She needs to feel your unrestrained love." Isabel gave her great-great-aunt a big hug and flashed her one of her best smiles.

It was around four o'clock in the afternoon when they returned to the town from Lem. Eliza, Fern, Ida, Mandy, and even Mr. Rodrigues went straight to the park. Isabel and her mother went home. Mrs. Rodrigues never went to the park. She would stay home and be joined by some of her cousins and friends. They would sit by the window, talk, and be entertained by the traffic of people in the park. Today there was such a crowd that people spilled out into the streets and the sidewalks around the park.

Isabel was looking out of the window, waiting for her friends to arrive, when all of a sudden, she yelled out to her mother, "Look, Mother! Look at them!" She pointed out the window in awe.

"Yes, Isabel. Everybody is here today. It is Easter Sunday."

"But look at Baba's feet. Look at Mr. Little-hands' hands, Mr. Tallman, and wow! Look at Miss Mary, Mother!" Isabel said.

A perplexed Mrs. Rodrigues responded, "Yes,

I see them Isabel! They are *who* they are," she spoke slowly, emphasizing "who they are."

Isabel realized that her mother was not seeing what she was seeing. Baba's feet were healed, and he was wearing brand new sandals, and he winked to Isabel as he passed by their window. Mr. Littlehands' hands were perfect, with long fingers, and he was playing the sweetest music that Isabel had ever heard. He nodded to Isabel as he passed by. Mr. Tallman, who was wearing a beautiful, silk, long robe, saluted to Isabel as he passed by, and Miss Mary had a white dress with a blue cape, and she was wearing a crown of white and pink flowers on her shiny, long hair. She smiled at her as she continued with her litany of Hail Marys.

"Are you okay, Isabel?" her mother asked, looking at her awestruck little daughter.

Isabel did not answer. She did not hear her mother and continued to stare out the window as if she were in a trance.

"Isabel! Isabel! Are you all right?" her mother asked, shaking her by the arm.

Isabel came to and responded, "I am fine, Mother. I was just thinking about something."

"Thinking about what?" her mother inquired.

"Oh, nothing. Nothing at all," she assured her mother. Quickly she added, "My friends are really late today. I wonder what is keeping them."

"Oh, they will come by and by. Probably they got held up by a late tea," her mother answered.

Isabel left her mother by the window and went to her room. She kissed the feet of Jesus on the little crucifix and said, "Thank you. Thank you."

She genuflected and blessed herself. She then went along the walls and touched the religious pictures in the house saying, "It is nice to have you back again."

She then ran to the backyard and to the peach tree. She crouched down and put her hand all the way into the hollow of the peach tree. There were no traces of the newspaper or anything else. The hollow was empty, clean and pristine. Then she noticed eggshells near her feet. She looked up, and perched in one of the higher branches of the tree was a nest filled with young *passarines*–birds of good news. The nest was unlike any other nest that she had ever seen. It was large, and woven in with the straw were gold and white stripes that looked liked ribbons. Sun-rays filtering among the trees lit the nest, and a gentle breeze rocked the branch lightly. The gold sparkled in and out, making its presence known. The mother *passarine* flew in with food, dropping some into each of the young warblers' gaping beaks. Then she began to fly, circling the nest and singing her song of good news.

Isabel was so mesmerized and enchanted by the bird's song that she did not hear her friends calling her in the distance.

"Isabel! Isabel! Where are you?" The voices became louder and louder as the girls entered the service side entrance. Just as they were about to open the door, Isabel came to and ran to meet them.

"Where have you been? We've been calling and calling you. Your mother said that you were around here," her friend Gloria said.

"I was just in the back, checking on something."

"Oh? Well, we are all set. Didija and the others are waiting," said Dee.

"Great!" Isabel exclaimed as she took the hands of her two friends and went running out towards the park. As she passed the house, she waved to her mother and her mother's friends in the window and then disappeared into the crowd.

The End

Author's Notes

[1] For more information about Vatican II, see *The Documents of Vatican II, All Sixteen Official Texts Promulgated by the Ecumenical Council, 1963–1965, translated from Latin.* Walter M. Abbott, S.J. General Editor and Very Rev. Msgr. Joseph Gallagher, Translation Editor, Guild Press, New York, 1966.

[2] For a complete and scholarly discussion of the historical background and the development of the Capeverdian Crioulo language and culture, see *Variation and Change in the Verbal System of Capeverdian.* Izione S. Silva, Ph.D. dissertation, Georgetown University, 1985.

[3] For a simple presentation of Martin Luther's story for children, see *Martin Luther, A Man Who Changed The World.* Paul Maier, Concordia Publishing house, 2004.

4   Carnival season begins in February and cul-
     minates on the Tuesday before Lent. Dur-
     ing Carnival, it is common to see people
     dress up as different characters with masks
     on. They are called "*mascaras*." The citing
     of "*mascaras*" creates excitement in town,
     as townspeople, especially children, follow
     them around and try to trick them in order to
     discover their true identities.

5   During the Carnival season, "pranks and
     tricks" were common. Some of these pranks
     were called '*assaltos*" when someone invari-
     ably steals something, like someone's supper.
     The objective is to discover who "stole" the
     object, but also that the person who stole the
     object returns it without being suspected.

6   Devotion to the Sacred Heart of Jesus prom-
     ises to bring peace to the family, blessing on
     all undertakings, and refuge at the hour of
     death. On December 27, 1673, a young visita-
     tion nun in Burgundy, France, named Marga-
     ret Mary Alacoque heard a strong inner voice
     that identified itself as Jesus Christ. Jesus

explained to her that He wanted His heart honored in the form of human flesh. He said to her, "Behold the heart which has so much loved men that it has spared nothing, even exhausting and consuming itself in testimony of its love." Jesus described to the young nun the image of His heart that He wanted painted. For more information on the devotion to the Sacred Heart of Jesus, see *Novena, the Power of Prayer.* Barbara Calamari and Sandra DiPasqua, Penguin Putnam Inc, New York, New York, 1999.

[7]   The rules and regulation for Ash Wednesday and for Lent have changed, and it is much more relaxed since Vatican II. Catholics of certain age are still required to fast on Ash Wednesday and on every Friday of Lent. During Lent, Catholics are also required to do penance by abstaining from eating or doing something that they love as a sacrifice, and also to give alms. For more information on this, please see, *Catechism of the Catholic*

Church second edition Libreria Editrice Vaticana, Citta del Vaticano, 1997.

[8] For further reading on the background of the theology presented in this chapter and elsewhere in this book, refer to:

1. *The Problem of Pain* by C.S.Lewis, HarperCollins, New York, 1996

2. *Heavenly Powers–unraveling the secret history of the Kabbalah* by Neil Asher Silverman, Castle Books, Edison, New Jersey, 2000.

3. *The Autobiography of St. Teresa of Avila, The life of St. Teresa of Jesus (1515–1582),* Tan Books and Publishers, Inc. Rockford ILL, 1997.

4. *The Story of a Soul–St. Térèse of Lisieux,* Michael Day, Mother Agnes of Jesus, TAN Books Publishers, Inc. Rockford ILL, 1997.

5. *Hail, Holy Queen,* Scott Hahn, Doubleday, New York, 2001.

6. *Diary, Divine Mercy in My Soul,* St. Maria Faustina Kowalska, Marians of the Immac-

ulate Conception, Stockbridge, Massachusetts, 2002.

7. *The King, Crucified and Risen–Medita-
tions on the Passion and Glory of Christ,*
Fr. Benedict Groeschel, C.F.R., Charis
Books, Servant Publications, Ann Arbor,
Michigan, 2002.

[9]   Vatican II also brought significant changes to
the Catholic Mass and to the look and feel
of the church. Most post-Vatican II churches
have few, or no, statues of the Saints at all.
The altar is fashioned as a table where the
priest faces the congregations as a community. People in the pews sing aloud with the
choir. Laity participates by giving out the
consecrated host and wine, reading the Scrip-
ture, and they have become the backbone of
the church's administration and teaching.

[10]   Catholic Church teaches the belief of the
"guardian angel." Each person at the time of
birth (or conception) is assigned a guardian
angel to protect and intercede for the person
during his/her sojourns on earth. For more

information on the Catholic teaching on guardian angels, see *Catechism of the Catholic Church,* second edition Libreria Editrice Vaticana, Citta del Vaticano, 1997.

[11] Willfully missing a Mass on Sunday, and on some holy days of obligation, is still considered a mortal sin in the Catholic Church. For more information about what constitutes 'mortal' and 'venial' sins, see *Catechism of the Catholic Church*, second edition Libreria Editrice Vaticana, Citta del Vaticano, 1997.

[12] The Catholic Church did not, in its canon, teach condemnation of Martin Luther. The Catholic Church, however, dealt harshly with Martin Luther. He was excommunicated, which meant that he was taken out from the communion in the Body of Christ, which is the gravest thing that can happen to a Catholic Christian. Folklore abounds about Martin Luther, and during pre-Vatican II days, the preaching of fire and brimstone was common. Protestantism was seen, still as late as the fifties, as the false and fallen church.

[13]   The Holy Week Traditions (for example, making of the Juda, killing of the spiders, and burning of the Judas) were folk p r a c-tices. Although not sanctioned by the Church, they were not discouraged, at least by the local church.

Contact Irma Silva-Barbeau
or order more copies of this book at

TATE PUBLISHING, LLC

127 East Trade Center Terrace
Mustang, Oklahoma 73064

(888) 361 - 9473

Tate Publishing, LLC

www.tatepublishing.com